DOWN ON THE
CHICKAHOMINY

DOWN ON THE
CHICKAHOMINY

THE LIFE AND
TIMES OF A
VANISHING
VIRGINIA RIVER

JACK TRAMMELL

Charleston London

THE
History
PRESS

Published by The History Press
Charleston, SC 29403
www.historypress.net

Copyright © 2009 by Jack Trammell, PhD
All rights reserved

Cover image: "Reflections of the Morning," by Tim Wilson, tawilsonphotography.com.

First published 2009

Manufactured in the United States

ISBN 978.1.59629.695.4

Library of Congress CIP data applied for.

CONTENTS

ACKNOWLEDGEMENTS

Special thanks must go to Randolph-Macon College for supporting this research. In particular, captain (and professor of biology) Dr. Art Conway has been a friend, mentor and constant inspiration for this project. In addition, my seven children and my wife, Audrie, have been extremely tolerant as I spent days away on the river or interviewing individuals. I tried to bring them to the river or the river back to them (we did eat some yellow perch to know what it tasted like). But most of all, this book is a result of Bill Buck's open hands and friendship and his infinite memories and love of life. I thank you all!

INTRODUCTION

America is blessed with many beautiful rivers, and First Americans, as well as later settlers, have universally been drawn to them for sustenance, transportation and protection and because they often appeal to something instinctual. Rivers are also centerpieces around which great natural beauty often accumulates.

The Chickahominy River is not among the famous of America's rivers; nor is it among the longest, widest or deepest. For the unique peoples who have lived along it, however, it is *the* river, and it gave birth to a unique culture that was intimately tied to the river's immediate environs. This unique river culture reached its zenith in the 1930s and 1940s, right up until the completion of Walker's Dam in 1943. In the minds of many, the dam changed everything—the fish, the water and even the "feel" of the river.

The living memories of those times are quickly disappearing. An opportunistic ethnographer seeks out as many primary sources as she or he can, capturing the memories, studying the artifacts and even living in the community. Even so, the effort is sometimes akin to trying to catch the wind in your hands. So much has already faded away.

But all good projects are born of good ideas, and it was Bill Buck's idea—when he found out that I liked to fish, wrote about history and sociology and was interested in the river—to tell me about this life and suggest that I interview others and preserve their experiences of the river. Over the course of three years, I increasingly became consumed with the story of the Chickahominy River, particularly in the World War II era. I began traveling to libraries, seeking out additional interviews with surviving community members and spending more time on and along the river.

At a certain point, I determined that I had to tell the story of the river.

Such was the goal of the Chickahominy Project. Bill Buck (often referred to as Buck in the text) and others like him grew up in a unique and insular water/river community along the Chickahominy during the Great Depression and World War II eras, a community that the inhabitants perhaps took for granted at the time but one that today seems very special, in some ways innocent, and very much focused on family and work in a way that might seem incongruous. It was a community tied to the water, quickly disappearing or changing as an observer moved inland in any direction. It was a truly unique Chesapeake Bay community.

It is a community that is now more or less extinct, precariously preserved in the memories of a few older individuals who connect the present to that past. In that not-so-distant past, individuals received their mail by boat, were married on the river (literally taking their vows in rolling Chickahominy flatboats), traveled to go Christmas shopping in Baltimore by river and sometimes were even transported to their graves by river.

Today, that community is difficult and sometimes impossible to find. The river has changed. It has become polluted and been cleaned up again; seen the proliferation of subdivisions and large river homes; experienced the loss of native species and the introduction of harmful nonnative species; and suffered the loss of many of its most familiar landmarks—fishing camps, riverside shack communities, fish houses and even most of the larger pre–World War II homes and riverside businesses like the brickyard.

Drawing on Bill's, Art's and many others' still extant memories, photographs, letters, primary documentary evidence and the remaining personal and intimate knowledge of the old river community captured in face-to-face interviews, this book attempts to highlight some of the key elements that made the Chickahominy river community so unique. It also tracks the history and environmental changes along the river and, melded with my own three years' experience on the river, attempts to weave a narrative thread with a "thick" description of what this community consisted of and meant.

This story will be interesting to the student of Virginia history and to those seeking to preserve the bay waterman's lifestyle. It will also appeal to readers who are interested in a collective past that is constantly in danger of being lost. But perhaps most importantly, it should serve as a reminder that change occurs at a pace that threatens our most important memories—even those of our presently living parents and grandparents, whom we sometimes inadvertently take for granted until they are taken away from us.

We must cherish and preserve their memories—these memories—and be more careful and cognizant in recording our own.

CHAPTER 1

BEGINNINGS AND ENDINGS

The founding of Jamestown in 1607 remains one of the great turning points in human history. On a small, low-lying peninsula in the lower James River, 105 Englishmen and boys landed and had no idea that they were changing the course of world events. They were more concerned with survival—45 or so of their comrades had already perished during the long Atlantic voyage. However, the tenuous foothold they established on a mosquito-ridden island was the seed of amazing and profound things to come.

Just up the river from the settlement was a confluence where another river joined the James. Called the Chickahominy by the local native Algonquin inhabitants, this tidal river was one of the first that European colonizers of Virginia explored after the initial settlement at Jamestown was established, and for a short time, it would share with the James a focal point in modern history. It was the river where the legendary Pocahontas swam, where natives caught a rich variety of aquatic life for food and other purposes and where they helped the English survive their first terrible winter. It was also where the famous (or infamous, depending on your perspective) Englishman John Smith was captured by men loyal to Pocahontas's father, Chief Powhatan, and held under a death sentence.

The Chickahominy river basin, along with its native inhabitants, soon faded into obscurity as the American colonies swiftly grew westward, fought for independence and emerged as a world superpower. Life along the Chickahominy, however, continued quietly in a fashion similar to the

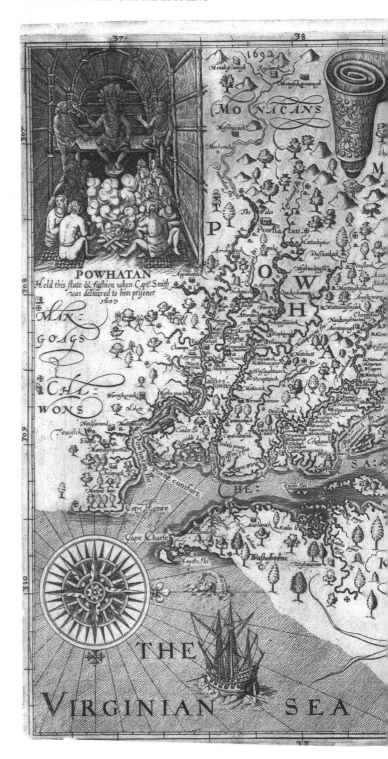

This map was created by information gathered in person by Captain John Smith and is one of the earliest of the Chickahominy region. *Courtesy of the Library of Congress.*

way it had for hundreds of years, and only in the face of profound twenty-first-century change and the threat of cultural extinction has interest in the river culture been resurrected. First Americans, English émigrés and African Americans have all left their marks on the Chickahominy; all now see a way of life permanently fading away, a way of life that still may have much to offer if it can be saved.

The original Chickahominy river culture *was* the Native American culture. Unlike other seminomadic eastern tribes, the Chickahominy Indians settled along the river in permanent villages where the environment was central to their everyday lives. Every resource that they harvested and utilized was connected to the river's ebb and flow, the climate and the cycles and geography of the tidal plain. Their villages were constructed along the river's higher sandy banks, near groves of white oak and native pines—these unique terrain features actually isolated and protected them from more aggressive and wide-ranging tribes, allowing them to perpetuate agriculture and a more settled lifestyle.

Then, as now, the river was tidal in its lower portions, a combination of fresh and salt water. The variety of animal life in and around the river was astonishing to the English settlers—crabs, oysters, clams, turtles, scallops and dozens of varieties of both saltwater and freshwater fishes. Ospreys, eagles and other waterfowl nested in cypress and fed in the marshes filled with beggar ticks, Indian oats and other grasses alongside the river's channels.

Ralph Hamor, an early settler, describes how the Chickahominies gave them "venison, turkeys, fresh fish, baskets, mats, and such like." The First Americans of the river were not wealthy in the material sense, but they were exceptionally wealthy by the natural standards of the river.

According to many personal accounts—those of several hundred years' past, as well as those right up until the construction of the dam in 1943—the water was clearer than in present times, and the bottom was quite sandy, particularly in the upper reaches.

The river is a short river by eastern U.S. standards, traveling roughly eighty miles from its headwaters west of the fall line to its wide meeting with the James. For the first few miles of the headwaters—north of Richmond along the Hanover County and Henrico County line—the Chickahominy is narrow and swampy, sometimes even difficult to distinguish in the surrounding marshy terrain. In this area west of the fall line, the water flows mainly over igneous and metamorphic bedrock, sometimes with a sandy bottom typical of other piedmont streams (like the North Anna River, for example). East of the fall line, near Mechanicsville, Virginia (where it passes beneath Interstate 95), the river becomes a coastal plains river, broadening and exhibiting a more heavily silted bottom, though it is still sandy on curves and on bars near the mouths of creeks. Farther east, past Providence Forge and the presently dammed Lake Chickahominy, the river becomes a tidal estuary, flowing directly into the James River and soon thereafter into the Chesapeake Bay.

During the Pleistocene Era (up until about ten thousand years ago), the river was much larger, with a much heavier water flow. The ancient banks are still identifiable in places, as are cutbacks and meander loops. During the most recent glacial period (approximately twenty thousand years ago), rising river levels contributed to backflows that have left today's marshes and flats all along the lower half of the river.

In the last ten thousand years, as man has utilized the region, the Chickahominy has consistently been a source of clean water and abundant aquatic life. Even before the settlement at Jamestown was established, and even before the Chickahominy tribe had established villages all along the banks of the river, mainly in what is today Charles City County, New Kent County and James City County, humans lived and survived along its banks. Using canoes that were slow-burned from single massive tree trunks, the Chickahominies were adept at multiple methods of harvesting from the river, including traps, nets, hooks, spears and even shot arrows. They were employing techniques that had evolved over thousands of years. Fish, crabs and oysters were commonly harvested.

The Chickahominy, however, was a river that soon would not be accessible to its longtime inhabitants. By the mid-eighteenth century, the original Chickahominy Indians, or "course pound corn people," had been forced northward, expelled from a reservation that they shared briefly with the Mattaponis and then literally written out of history by white historians like Thomas Jefferson. Today, the surviving Chickahominy descendants still suffer from a legacy of neglect and discrimination.

The Chickahominies, like their home river, were and are a unique phenomenon. Whether in comparison to other tribes or to the new white settlers, they were a remarkably democratic social unit, governed by a council of eight leaders rather than a single chief. They relied on consensus-making and were generally a peaceful tribe, even among their more warlike neighbors. In fact, despite their association with Chief Powhatan, they refused to become subjects beneath anyone.

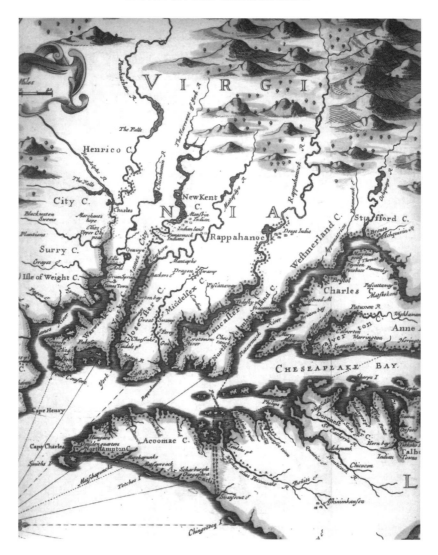

This map, produced in 1676, shows details of the Chickahominy region. *Courtesy of the author.*

John Smith described the first Chickahominy village he encountered:

> [It] *lay a quarter mile from the river, containing thirty or forty houses, upon an exceeding high land; at the foot of the hill towards the river, is a plain wood, watered with many springs, which fall twenty yards down right into the river. Right against the same is a great marsh, of four or five miles circuit, divided in two islands, by the parting of the river, abounding with fish and fowl of all sorts.*

Unfortunately, the Chickahominies were ill-equipped to deal with the inevitable clash between Powhatan's confederation and the growing colonial population. In 1614, the Chickahominies signed a treaty with Sir Thomas Dale, whereby the natives agreed to supply corn and warriors and Dale agreed to let them remain semiautonomous. This was the first in a long line of one-sided agreements between the settlers and the First Americans.

The peace with the Chickahominies lasted for only a brief time, and by 1622 the fragile and misunderstood agreement had shattered. All agreements made with the colonists were unfair to the natives at best, as the newcomers attempted to cut against the grain and convert the natives to Christianity and force them to adopt their social customs. At the celebration of the 1614 treaty, Ralph Hamor summarized this attitude: "[They] became as familiar amongst us as if they had been Englishmen indeed."

But they were not Englishmen. After the 1622 massacre, English settlers began to push westward along both banks of the Chickahominy. By 1646, a new treaty had relegated the Chickahominies to reservations in King William near the York River, many miles distant from their original home. Although a 1669 census lists Chickahominies living in New Kent County (part of the northern bank of the Chickahominy River), their villages were removed from the river and the land had been taken over for cultivation and settlement.

The Chickahominy diaspora, which began officially in 1702 when they were forced out of King William, led some to believe that the tribe had literally become extinct. Thomas Jefferson declared so (erroneously) in 1781. In fact, it was soon thereafter when a gradual migration began back to the river, and after more than three hundred years, the Chickahominies again own communal land along the river (this happened in 2002 for the eastern division of the tribe, the Chickahominy Indians Easter Division, or CIED).

During the 1930s and 1940s, when Bill Buck and others were growing up along the river, there were Chickahominies living in the river community, but they were second-class citizens, amalgamated into the category of "black" by government agencies and denied their own identity. One man in particular, Dr. Walter Plecker, was determined to erase native Virginians through "documentary genocide." Plecker promoted the Racial Integrity Act of 1924 and other attempts to erase native heritage. In 2001 and 2007, the Virginia General Assembly finally expressed "profound regret" for the oppression of Virginia natives, including Hitleresque racial purity laws, but most modern Chickahominies still feel the sting of policies that were in place for hundreds of years.

Few physical remains are left from the seventeenth century. There is still some wilderness along the riverbanks that is much the same as the terrain was in 1607. *Courtesy of the author.*

Between the eastern tribe and the Charles City tribe, there are presently about one thousand Chickahominies in eastern Virginia. Chief Gene Pathfollower Adkins, CIED, has made his mission federal recognition of the Chickahominy tribe. The state recognized the tribe officially in 1983, but because of the great diaspora, the federal government and the Bureau of Indian Affairs have placed obstacles at every turn, to this point denying formal federal recognition.

"Those of us who lived in the forest are non-reservated," Chief Adkins explained in an interview. "We were hoping that Jamestown [2007 celebration in Virginia] would change things…We don't want a reservation. We just want federal recognition."

The story of the Chickahominies is not always a happy one, and rightly or wrongly, blacks and whites living along the river in the 1930s and 1940s were notably unaware of, or indifferent to, it. Aside from sometimes attending or noting the annual powwow held at Windsor Shades by the remnant of the tribe, they paid little attention to natives.

"We knew some Indians when I was growing up," T.R., a childhood friend of Buck's, said during an interview. Bill confirmed this, but neither had much more to say about it.

The Native American notion of property ownership was never consistent with the legal system of surveys and registered deeds that the newcomers brought to the administration of the New World. After the diaspora, farms and occasional plantations sprang up on the north and south banks of the Chickahominy, as did small wharves and independent fisheries. At Shipyard Point, a small shipbuilding industry formed, important during the Revolutionary War.

A commercial fishing industry sprang up almost immediately, as it did elsewhere around the rich Chesapeake Bay region. Although no commercial centers or cities arose, in part due to the terrain, villages did appear and often included a tavern, sometimes a forge or metal shop and several surrounding homes.

Some of the early history of the river, difficult to find in documentary evidence, survives in place names suggestive of early functions and environment: Fish House Landing, Persimmon Bay, Smith Island (where Captain John Smith was captured by warriors of Powhatan), Edwards Mill, Pine Landing, Buzzard Island, Oak Tree Landing, Sycamore Springs and Barrett's Ferry.

Some of the names used in the 1930s and 1940s are neither found on modern maps (such as those made for popular use by GMCO) nor on older maps lacking greater detail. Bill has tried to pass those names on: Menzel's Creek (Uncle Neck Creek), Bush Neck Creek (Nettles Creek), Marshies Creek (Morris Creek), Pigs Point and Blanks Point (Pig Point and Blank Point—without the *s*) and Hog Neck Creek (Lobbs Creek), to mention only a few. Bill, T.R., Art and others can point out many other "mistakes" made by modern cartographers of the region.

Moreover, the landscape has changed considerably over the four hundred years or so of recorded history. The big white house where Bill grew up, built by his grandfather and other locals about 1893, is located on what is today called Old Neck Point near Big Stump Creek. During the Civil War, however, the area that is today Buck's old house and surrounding farm and woodland was part of a large, swampy, uninhabited island—the river has literally shifted course by more than a mile south to north, turning an island into a landlocked point (actually a neck). This is in part why there are so few physical traces of the First American or white

The Chickahominy River as it appeared to an eighteenth-century artist. *Courtesy of the author*.

College of William and Mary archaeologists excavated a native village on Old Neck at the Buck home. *Courtesy of the author.*

settler Chickahominy cultures—the landscape around the river is subject to dramatic changes over time.

Interestingly, College of William and Mary archaeologists did locate and excavate a native village near and on Buck's old homestead, after Buck had left home to join the air force. According to Charles City County authorities, "During the late 1960s…a paled Chickahominy site was excavated. The site was located on Old Neck Road and is believed to be associated with the village labeled Mansa on the Don Pedro de Zuniga map." Buck has many pictures of these excavations, which his family took at the time. Given the changing nature of the landscape, such finds must be considered good fortune.

Native place names also have survived into the present: Possum (Run), Tonyham (Run/Swamp), Muskout (Run/Island), Wickwa (Bridge)—John Smith recorded a native bridge over the river, which this might be named for—and Tanks Paspahegh (Creek). Of course, the name Chickahominy itself is an anglicized adaptation of an Algonquin word.

Other history is preserved in odd, out-of-the-way places: a two-zloty Polish coin commemorating Polish artisans who arrived in Jamestown and the Chickahominy area in 1608 or even fiberglass canoes that are omnipresent in middle-class American garages or behind back porches (and directly

Marsh flowers on the Chickahominy River. *Courtesy of the author.*

descended from native vessels made from single tree trunks burned hollow). In particular, the human power of naming, bestowed in one tradition by God in the Old Testament, preserves places and their memories even when the physical signs no longer remain. When mapmakers came through the region in the 1960s and 1970s, many place name mistakes were made. Old-timers still resent that very much.

Bill cryptically commented in one interview: "It's not history until someone cares about it."

Local names are quickly lost when the people move or pass away. Bill and others have supplied a literal lexicon of such local terms, including unusual names like willow cat (a small channel catfish); mud gobbler (a large channel catfish); old fork tail (any channel catfish); Mississippi cats (white catfish); red darners (a local type of dragonfly); rose mallow (a marsh flower); ivy (a rhododendron-type plant with inner wood that appears to be like ivory); or kickers (small-horsepower boat engines).

Why so many names for the channel catfish?

"The channel cat is the beauty of the family, I think," Bill said, smiling.

For those individuals living in the water community in the 1930s and 1940s, all of this history dating back to 1607 and beyond was present but blurry, like all of the highlights of the current. It was passed along mainly in stories from older relatives and in the shared experience of the river itself.

This was the world into which Buck, T.R. and many others were born.

CHAPTER 2

BORN TO THE RIVER

Bill is a product of the river. Born on January 17, 1942, in a big white house on the river, his oldest memories always include the river, and the deepest human associations in his life are with people who grew up along, lived near or worked on the river. In the present, one standing near him can imagine that the river is literally on him somehow, that the stains on his work pants are from the water, mud and flotsam of the river and that the faded color in his hat was burned away by the reflection of the afternoon Virginia sun on the river. Or perhaps the river may be better said to be in him; somehow, water from the Chickahominy flows through his veins.

Buck, however, was somewhat glib and nonchalant when asked about it.

"This river is where I grew up." He shrugged. "I suppose I know a little about it."

Captain Art Conway had a similar reaction. "I know a little bit about the river," he said, with the slightest of smiles. Conway was raised near Kilmarnock on the Chesapeake Bay, on an inlet five miles from town, and grew into young adulthood as a commercial fisherman. From the 1970s onward, he has fished and, more recently, guided on the lake portion of the Chickahominy River above Walker's Dam.

"This is where us river pirates were born!" T.R. said, pointing to the river and making reference to many teenage escapades, some of which still remain secret.

Bill as a youngster, with his mother, grandfather and Uncle Penny around the big white house. *Courtesy of Captain Bill Buck Jr.*

The Chickahominy, though a relatively short river, dominates the geography along its winding route. From its swampy origins in Hanover County to its half-mile-wide confluence with the James River near Colonial Williamsburg and the Jamestown Settlement, it reaches out in countless swamps, creeks and guts (small tidal fingers of water that rise and fall in creeks connected to the river) deep into the land on either side. The section where Bill grew up—the lower third of the river—is wide and sometimes deep, with all of the characteristics of a larger navigable tidal river. In some places, the opposite shore remains hazy and flat on the distant horizon half a mile or more away. In other places, even a full quarter mile from any land, you can jump out of the boat and twist your ankle landing on the sandy bottom less than one foot below the water's surface. Subtle but powerful currents play with the tide and can suddenly push a boat off course. When a south–east wind blows in against a hard outgoing tide, standing waves can abruptly turn the river into white caps and deep troughs that distract even veteran boaters.

Along this stretch of a short, but in some ways very big, river, Bill Buck grew up spending more time on the water than on dry land. Using the big white farmhouse (still in the family) right on the bank of the river as a base of operations, he used a Chickahominy boat (a unique combination of flatboat and keeled skiff) to meet friends, pole into remote creeks, check crab pots and nets or just stay on the water. He used unique Chickahominy paddles handcrafted by his grandfather, with Walker Potter's help, out of local white oak.

He wasn't alone. In the 1930s and into the 1940s, busy barge traffic still plied up and down the lower half of the river. Mail traveled across the river. Materials like glass and tin used to finish the big white house came by river and Chickahominy boat. Barrels were floated across the river from point to point. Cattle were moved on barges and flatboats. Chickahominy boats were strung together, covered with crude decking and used to drive hogs across the river. Commercial fishermen set nets for various freshwater and saltwater species.

Lily pads, mainly the yellow pond lily (*Nuphar lutea*), covered the river from near the James all the way up into the narrow Hanover County channel, often in fields of several hundred acres or more. The shoreline of the Chickahominy was largely wooded, punctuated by small fishing shacks, wharves, an occasional house and several large businesses, including Menzel's Fish House near the brickyard where huge quantities of fresh fish and shellfish were processed every season and shipped to northern markets. The remains of Menzel's Fish House were torn down during the making of the Disney movie *Pocahontas*.

The culture of those who lived along the river was distinct and unique. Extending perhaps a mile or two inland on either side of the river, the people who lived along the Chickahominy in New Kent County, James City County and Charles City County enjoyed an insular existence that was oriented toward the water and the small number of local acquaintances or relatives who shared their livelihoods and connections to the water. Bill's memories of his childhood along the river, like other longtime residents interviewed, included a mixture of things that they saw, as well as things about which they were told. When Bill's grandfather was alive, to cite just one example, Bill heard him talk about local events in the first person, dating back to as long ago as the Civil War. Bill and others like him provide a rich repository of living cultural information that cannot always be proven factually but is undeniably an important part of the reality of the river culture.

"I was born right down on the river. My granddad had that house built [the big white house across from Big Marsh Point]. I was raised like Robert Ruark [a reference to *The Old Man and the Boy*]."

"You know Route 5," Bill said,

> *it crosses the river at what used to be called Barrett's Ferry. Of course it was replaced with the bridge* [Barrett's Ferry Bridge was built in 1939 and replaced in 2009]. *Route 5 was a gravel wagon trail before the depression, and my dad worked on the CCC* [Civilian Conversation Corps] *making it into a paved road. Between the land, the river, and the garden, we were never hurting for anything. But we did need cash. My dad told me how the foreman would unlock the tool box every morning, and the guys would fight for the tools. You see, no tool, no work; no work, no pay.*

From a very early age, Bill spent an enormous amount of time on the water. He recalls coming down the river as a child on one of the family's Chickahominy boats to see the new bridge. Most of all, however, he remembers the boat:

> *The Chickahominy boat is a little different from other bay boats. It's unique in my experience. It was not a true flatboat, or a true keeled boat, but had*

The 1939 construction of Barrett's Ferry Bridge for Route 5. Note what appears to be a Chickahominy boat tied up to the left. *Courtesy of the CCHC.*

The Hofmeyer girls of the lower river in a James River boat. *Courtesy of the CCHC.*

elements of both. They were built locally, of course, and had to be soaked to seal the joints. In the 1940s, there was a minimum of two of these at every household along the river—they were used for everything.

Chickahominy boats are part of a wonderful collection of unique small craft original to the bay and its tributaries. Many of these boats are now lost to history. "A rich variety of indigenous Chesapeake small craft evolved from...necessity," William Warner wrote in the *Beautiful Swimmers*, describing this phenomenon.

"Diascund Creek boats were different," Bill said. "The Lenexa boats were a little different. You won't find any of these Chickahominy boats anymore."

The Chickahominy boats are now gone. Only one is extant to Bill's knowledge, holding potted plants in front of an old seafood restaurant along Route 60 near Richmond. Bill would also take his Chickahominy boat into the marshy creeks near the big white house where he grew up, still a family residence across from Big Marsh Point. Buck and other young men fished, swam and hunted ducks and other fowl in the numerous creeks—Uncle Penny's Creek, Parsons Creek, Shipyard Creek—delighting

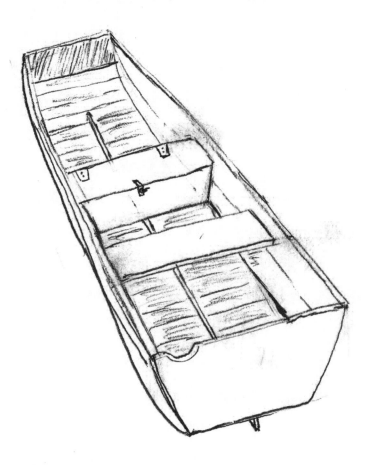

A sketch of a Chickahominy boat by the author, based on descriptions.

in the solitude, the closeness to nature and the freedom. When they caught something big enough, or enough of it, they were also likely to take it downriver to one of the fish markets, like Menzel's Fish House, to pick up a little bit of extra cash.

"If you hung a really large one," Bill recalled, "you took it to the country store for bragging rights."

T.R. remembers rescuing a Chickahominy boat as a teenager.

"I resurrected an old Chickahominy boat," he said in an interview. "Each side was one piece, usually cypress. You had to keep water in the bottom of the boat so the swelling would keep the boards sealed. We put it in the truck and got it home and fixed it up."

Buck, T.R., Ricky Ray, Doug, Petey and many other boys their age spent practically all their time on or near the river. On another occasion, Buck found a Chickahominy boat in the trash pile at the Smith Island Marina and pulled it out to repair and salvage.

"Rarely two days went by without the river," T.R. said. "The river was like eating and drinking."

Bill's mother taught him how to go out on the high tide with worms and a cane pole and to drift with the current through the lily pads, catching perch, bass and crappie. She always packed biscuits, cornbread or what Bill remembers as "batter bread" (probably similar to hush puppies). When she fried the fish at night, he remembers "sliced tomatoes from the garden and hot biscuits and ice tea. What an end to a wonderful day!"

The boys would often have races along the river, using ten-horsepower outboards with fourteen-foot johnboats. As the fields of lily pads died down in the late summer and fall, they would increasingly cut corners and take shortcuts to gain an advantage.

"T.R. turned his boat over once doing that," Bill said.

"Sometimes when I was at Bill's house," T.R. recalled, "I would look across the river, and on the hill to the left I could see Mount Airy; to the right, I could see the stacks at the brickyard and to the west I could see Uncle Penny's mill."

"You might go out," Bill recalled, "and not see another boat for the entire day, or even another house."

Buck and many others also remember the amazing, wide-ranging fields of lily pads in the river that sometimes covered several hundred acres in a single location. The disappearance of the pads in the early 1990s, almost completely missing below the dam by 2005, has perplexed many observers. An invisible line between Old Neck and Big Marsh seems to be the divide between no pads and a few pad fields below the lake. Even in 2009, when some pads have reappeared in the lake above the dam, the population still appears in danger.

Nevertheless, the vegetation of the region still remains diverse and lush. Along the river and marshes and in shallow water, wild rice, arrow arum, cattails, pickerelweed and cordgrass grow. The rice was harvested hundreds of years earlier by the Chickahominies. In the creeks, button bushes, alders and yellow irises flourish. Most of all, the bald cypress, often used for making roof shingles, dots the banks along the lower half of the river and dominates the river scenery. Bald eagles and ospreys are fond of nesting in the tops of cypress. A study in 1980 by College of William and Mary researchers found almost fifty major species of marsh plant life alongside or in the river.

The themes that reoccurred across all of the interviews, and particularly with the primary subject, Bill Buck, were themes that included the centrality of family, hard work and the richness of the river. There was also a degree of humility and privacy among the individuals, not any kind of inhospitality to speak of, but rather akin to the reserved humility found in the Scotch-Irish settlers of Appalachia who value family loyalty and circumspection among strangers. Most individuals interviewed did not speak much about deeply personal conflicts, sensitive issues of race or other delicate matters, unless it was in general terms. The same could unequivocally be said of all the First Americans interviewed, in spite of other more obvious cultural differences with whites and blacks.

Still, Bill told some stories with hushed irreverence, pretending to be embarrassed but obviously delighted to share the story. When I asked him about his grandparents again, another story came to his mind:

> My granddad took the wagon one time before I was born on a trading trip, and my grandmother specifically asked him to bring back a butter churn. We were pretty self-sufficient, but still needed sugar, glass, things like that. Well he came back, so I'm told, more than a little drunk, but he did indeed have the butter churn. My grandmother stormed out to the wagon and found the whiskey bottle and broke it against a tree. My granddad then took the butter churn and smashed it into pieces. There were men working on the house, and a silence fell over everything. Three days later, he set out in the wagon again. He came back with another butter churn. This time, she broke it on the pile of bricks the workers were using! I'm sure those workers were trying very hard not to laugh.

Bill's grandfather cut railroad ties and sold them, and sometimes Bill worked for him. The Southern Railway would buy them for fifty cents a tie. Back in the 1920s, there had been a thriving industry for railroad ties, which were cut from the riverbank, stacked next to the river and transported by barge to Newport News or other destinations. Sometimes crude rafts of cedar trees tied together would serve as small barges, and Bill remembers seeing them tied in groups along the river. By the 1960s, many had sunk, and there was good fishing in their midst for crappie and other pan fish.

A sunken barge from the days when traffic was heavy on the river. *Courtesy of the author.*

Bill's childhood also included formal education, which at one point involved a one-hour bus ride to an all-white school in Charles City and a half-mile walk each way to and from the bus stop. There were also years spent in a one-room country schoolhouse. Bill credits learning to read with changing his life.

"I love to read," he said many times.

> *I don't know where I'd be if I hadn't learned to read. That's made all the difference to me. I used to go to my grandmother's room, and she would read aloud for long periods of time. I would just sit there and listen. She would read all kinds of things to me, including newspapers that we would get.*

Much later, when she passed away, Bill personally dug her grave site at the cemetery in Holdcroft, where other family members also rested.

The older residents interviewed for this project all have vivid memories of the World War II period, along with photographs, diaries and letters, but very few have actual relics from their time on the vibrant river itself. This begs a question an anthropologist might ask: since we have archaeology of the dirt and anthropology of the village, how do we capture a people of the water, who leave behind neither bones nor structural remains in the classic sense? The current of the river has literally carried away the ripples left by their presence and without physical objects on the bed of the river, what traces can one dig for? What memory beyond living memories can be traced?

All of the living Chickahominy residents from the 1930s and 1940s remember the construction of Walker's Dam in 1943 as a seminal event in the life of the river community. Many Chickahominy Indians believe that it destroyed the river. Bill has few memories of his own of the river before the dam but also countless stories handed down to him by others. These stories included annual shad runs on par with those in the James and Appomattox Rivers; net catches that could hold five hundred pounds of large yellow perch at one time; and fishing along the "grand bank" for grey trout and spot. All of this changed when the dam was built and created Chickahominy Lake, cutting the tidal river in half to serve the World War II industrial and residential water needs of Newport News.

Bill was still young when this happened and would row the Chickahominy boat back to the big white house while his mother cleaned the fish that they had caught moments earlier in Parsons Creek right in the back of the boat. The dam was just above their home, and though the river remained tidal below it, the river was always different after its construction. Bill remembers the remains of a large plantation home on Parson's Island—there is nothing remaining there now, save a cypress stump. No remains, no ruins; nothing but trees and a blackened cypress stump.

"This river has been dead in my time," Chief Gene Pathfollower Adkins of CIED said during an interview. Many Chickahominies, the First Americans of the river, still live along it, though few can make their living from it anymore.

"Newport News Waterworks destroyed the river," Jerry Adkins, assistant chief of CIED, agreed. Many Chickahominies had formerly made their living fishing the river, dating back to pre-colonial times.

"Oh, it changed the river, of that I have no doubt," Bill said. "The dam killed the shad run. And the locals were upset. My father [William Buck Sr.] never talked too much about it. But some people threatened to dynamite it." He shook his head after saying this. "There are so many things that make [the river] different [now]."

Bill remembers that his father sailed to Baltimore, hauling bricks from the local brickyard down the Chickahominy on a three-masted schooner, past Newport News, actually outrunning the train from Lenexa in a sailing ship. From the big white house, Bill could hear the whistle when the shift changed at the brickyard, and sometimes he even heard the gondolas pulled by mules moving back and forth into and out of the woods where clay was collected or bricks stacked. At low tide one day, Bill pointed out that many bricks can still be seen at the old site, which now has an ordinary campground, a boat ramp and not much else. An osprey had nested in the top of an old crane near the end of a rotting pier. As a child, Bill would take a Chickahominy boat past here to get the mail, to get an ice cream farther downriver or just to fish or hunt.

"I remember catching bullfrogs by hand with Bill during breeding season," T.R. said in an interview. "His mom made a bullfrog platter. I pretty much lived at Bill's house."

Lewis Jester reported that in 1944, "natives [made] excellent money out of the [frog] business. The frogs [were] blinded with a bright light and easily…picked up (hundreds of dozens of jumbo frogs) as one [stalked] them in a flat-bottom boat."

There were also many memories for local residents that are not so pleasant to document or talk about. Bootlegging whiskey, for example, involved large sums of money for the times, and the sale of mason jars and sugar was closely monitored. Home distilling was widely practiced and generally tolerated by locals (and the brew was commonly imbibed), but it is still talked about in hushed tones today. One hot day when Bill, T.R. and other childhood friends were sitting in school, which of course had no air conditioning, they heard a series of loud booms through the open window. They later confirmed that it was stills being blown up. The teacher looked at them sternly, saying, "Turn around! Y'all know what's going on."

T.R. recalled how men came to buy all of his father's rancid peaches.

"I didn't understand at first why these men would come in a truck and spend money on all the rotten and dead peaches—they were making peach brandy!"

Life remained simple, even as creature comforts like refrigerators, televisions and indoor plumbing slowly made their way into more households.

"Even a fan was high tech!" T.R. said.

Bill remembers telephone and electric service coming to the river in his childhood. The electric line followed the main road to Holdcroft but did not branch out into hard-to-reach areas unless customers were willing to pay "by the pole" to have it installed. The cost was prohibitive.

But then the state said "give the people power," and all of a sudden my mother was boarding and feeding a crew of workmen. There were six to eight of them in each room.

Later, the C&P telephone company installed our first phone. It was a party line—if it rang twice it was for you; if it rang once it was for the neighbor. I remember the first television, with tubes of course, and rushing through my chores to watch Howdy Doody.

In 1961, a septic system with indoor plumbing was installed just as Bill was heading off to service in the air force. It was about that time that he and his family members took their first "hot showers" in the sense that modern Americans take for granted. The outhouse had always been behind the barn, and a bath had always meant boiling water and dumping it into a tub.

Almost all individuals interviewed remembered working in large family gardens, in hot fields of corn or beans or in orchards. And, of course, on the water.

"When we weeded beans, I remember dad forcing us to keep taking salt pills," T.R. recalled, not sounding very nostalgic.

Most young men along the river learned at an early age to skull, an art that Bill believes is being lost. He recalled that his uncle Arthur Penny, another true waterman, "finally agreed to take me fishing with him." It is one of Bill's earliest and most enduring memories.

"My mom finally said okay, and he tied a rope around my waist and tied the other end to the boat. It probably wasn't too safe."

Uncle Penny, among many other things, taught Bill how to flat skull a boat, how to set a catfish pot, how to "read" a "gut" (analyze the marshy inlets in the tidal flats for depth and cover-holding fish) and how to always fish the deep side of a creek.

Uncle Penny was also a market hunter who shipped game birds to Baltimore.

"He was a hard old man," Buck recalled.

But he made an impression on me. My Uncle Penny was a very serious fisherman. When he was working that net, you didn't say much; you just watched. He was very, very good. Those were some of the best years of my life.

Uncle Penny, in addition to a regular house, had a houseboat that he kept on the river, and he also built a cabin in the woods nearby. The houseboat eventually sank, and parts of it ended up in the construction of a landing known as Arthur Penny's Landing. He taught his nephew an incredible array of facts about the river.

Bill also learned from his father, who had a Parker twelve-gauge double-barrel shotgun, with steel twisted barreling and Trojan-grade metal with which his son was very fascinated. Buck Sr. often hunted with dogs and even enjoyed traditional English foxhunts.

Bill, T.R., Art and others also learned the wisdom of the water that does not come from books:

> *When the first flake of snow falls, pull the pots—not another fish will go in.*
> *We all get gilled, man and fish alike, soon or late.*
> *When the male ospreys are here, then spring is quite near.*
> *If the ivy* [a local version of mountain laurel] *is blooming, the turtles are crawling.*
> *If you find a tree the cormorants are roosting in you have found a bonanza and a bountiful catch is almost guaranteed.*

Bill remembers in vivid detail how the special paddles for Chickahominy boats were made—information that cannot be found in any book. He knows the names of countless small creeks and inlets that have no names (or incorrect names) on modern maps. He remembers reading *Four Years under Marse Robert* when he was ten and being told that his ancestor Deacon Richard Buck came to Jamestown and married John Rolfe and Pocahontas. He remembers having a strange combination of fear and respect for his father:

> *I remember dad walking across the field to the last bend in Dick News Creek to catch a mess of bream for dinner. The bull-heads (catfish) congregated here to eat the bream eggs. Every time my dad caught one* [instead of a bream], *he would say words that are not for publication, and throw it as far across the creek as he could. However, when my dad was not along, my mother took the mighty bull-heads and prepared them for supper, and dad always ate them with gusto.*

Bill remembers that his father was an endless source of knowledge to his young son:

My dad had an eye for a straight-grained white oak tree. He and my granddad would take a two-man crosscut saw, cut a ten-foot section, use a wedge and split the heart out, then hang the pieces on the north side of the barn with weights hanging on the bottom of them to eventually make them into Chickahominy paddles. There never was a piece that split.

Bill has several of these vintage paddles; unique, slender, long and finely worked, they are part paddle, part oar and part pole, depending on the need. "Call it a paddle, not an oar," Bill said. "They were used for sculling."

When the wood was ready, we would take it to Walker Potter, who also gave fifty-cent haircuts. He would lay a pattern on it, use an asp to get it square, and then use a hand-held jigsaw and drawing knife to shape it. Later he would scrap it with glass, and then apply four coats of linseed oil. [Bill smiled.] He would charge five dollars per paddle.

Bill's father, in addition to being an accomplished waterman, also knew his trees and passed that knowledge along to his son. Eventually, Bill would run his own nursery and have his own specialized knowledge of trees.

"He would look at trees and say, 'this one's for firewood' or 'this one is going to split easy,' or he might note a squirrel's nest. Of course, he would rather squirrel hunt than eat."

It goes without saying that Bill's father knew the river well. He would take Bill and his mother to an obscure point at the end of some lily pads, no more than six feet deep, that was a channel catfish hot spot during certain times of the year.

"I can remember this as if it was today," Bill wrote in his own notes.

My father carried a twenty-foot cane pole which he stuck in the mud to tie the boat to. Mother's float slipped below; a large tail appeared; dad untied the boat and the chase was on. After fifteen minutes or so, dad reached and grabbed the fish through the gills. [It was] a monster by anyone's standards.

At a certain point, Bill's father decided that his son must learn to master the art of handling a Chickahominy boat. Buck Sr. came home with a two-hundred-foot length of rope, one end of which he tied to a tree beside the water and the other end to a boat. He put one paddle in the boat.

"'Get on board,' he told me. After some instruction, I was allowed to skull the boat the distance the rope would let me go. He gave me a stern warning not to untie the rope without his permission."

Bill recalled in an interview that practice was unlimited. "Every day after school, chores and homework, it was to the river." It seemed like it took forever, and it was one of the few times he recalls being unsure of himself. Finally, he felt ready.

Dad calmly untied the rope and pushed the boat hard out into the river. Instead of rushing off, I calmly sculled the boat back to him. After all these years I can still remember the smile on his face. Many years later, mother told me that he would walk up behind a cedar tree on top of the hill and watch my progress.

None of the families of individuals interviewed were wealthy back in the 1930s and 1940s, or even middle class by contemporary standards, yet they were never wanting for anything.

"I don't know how she did it sometimes," Buck said, "but my mother always had food around. Even when other workers or family members showed up, we always had food. Back then, out in the country, we took a lot of meals off the land."

Stuart, a longtime tow truck driver in New Kent County, said almost the exact same thing. "I don't know how we did it. But we always had food. We often fed as many as twelve people at dinner. We had a huge garden, too."

The river provided a seemingly endless supply of some foodstuffs. Foods that now seem like great delicacies to those who live even a few dozen miles away—fresh crab, flounder, oysters, mussels, wild duck, rockfish, shad, herring, perch; the list goes on and on. Yet the people who lived there saw the region as beautiful but not grand or privileged.

"The Chesapeake does not impress those who know it best as the grandest or most of anything," William Warner wrote in the *Beautiful Swimmers*. "For all its size and gross statistics, it is an intimate place where land and water intertwine in infinite varieties of mood and pattern."

Bill and his family and friends were unpresumptuous, and they were certainly on intimate terms with their physical environment.

Bill's childhood world also included religion at the nearby Baptist church in Holdcroft (to offset the "bad habits" that Uncle Penny taught him), trips to the Orange & Walker general store to get candy and basic supplies and, beyond that, work, work and more work.

The big white house as it appears in the present. *Courtesy of Captain Art Conway*.

The College of William and Mary excavations of a Chickahominy village site, literally on Buck's homestead. *Courtesy of Captain Bill Buck Jr.*

"My world was so small then," Bill said in one interview, reflecting backward. "And I was a son to many men [he was a young man constantly around older men working on the river]."

Bill was the youngest and only male of four children and, as such, was accorded much privilege from his father. He helped his father fish, cut and stacked firewood and constantly worked in the garden. His father, William T. Buck Sr., was also an accomplished horseman and passed knowledge along to Bill about handing horses and managing money.

"My father was quite a horseman," Bill said. "He could pop a ring at a gallop. He dated my mother in an old-fashioned horse-and-buggy. He also rode foxhound."

For Bill, however, the 1939 Chevy pickup truck was the only proper means of transport:

> *Things were remote then. I learned to drive my dad's pickup truck. They gave driver's tests once a month in Providence Forge, and I remember getting a black-and-white piece of paper, with no photo on it. There was no law. There was a sheriff, but he didn't have any deputies. We didn't need any law.*

The eastern Chickahominies near the river at that time built the Samaria School, a one-room schoolhouse that was destined to change many lives for the better.

"My mother, who would be ninety-three, went to school there," Chief Adkins said.

Adkins and others can relate stories of the river from that time: how tribe members could walk half a mile across the river on ice and cut blocks from it to fill icehouses (Bill and others remember this amazing winter event, including watching ice pile up during the change of tides, an event that has not occurred again since the construction of the dam); how baptisms regularly were carried out in the waters of the river (and later how white shirts always came out very brown); how tribe members could support themselves solely from the wealth of the river (Gene's grandfather was a commercial fisherman before the dam); and, in a less pleasant way, how natives were treated as second-class citizens.

"People would cross the street not to speak to Indians," Adkins said.

Blacks, too, were subject to a post–Civil War southern system that adhered in principle to separate but equal but in practice to separate and unequal services. During one journey around the overgrown riverbanks, Bill stopped and talked somberly in the midst of a group of large white oak trees and a vague road trace.

"This was a shantytown where blacks lived," he said quietly. "A tar paper village. There's nothing left now, but at the time there were a dozen or more little shacks here. They worked various small jobs, including some who were fishermen. I knew some of them."

Bill, T.R. and other longtime residents are forced to remember one system in which they grew up and reconcile it with a completely different system in which their grandchildren live now. They often choose not to talk about this aspect of the river community, not because of any latent prejudices, but simply because it is awkward. It is human nature to refrain from throwing out the good memories of earlier years in order to satisfy a curious present. Most of the memories, however, are indeed pleasant, and most are intimately connected to the river and the river culture.

Art remembers duck hunting on the river in the 1970s. T.R. can't forget much of the mischief he has gotten into along the river. Edwin remembers the river stories that his older family members talked about frequently. Jacqueline remembers how different life was seventy-five years ago, everywhere in Virginia but particularly in the Chickahominy region. R.R. remembers the food his mother cooked, the like of which he hasn't had in forty years or more.

"When I grew up," Bill said, "I listened to these people. I have retained all of that stuff. I tried to take it in because I was interested in it, but now kids…don't take it in."

Part of what the kids don't "take in," as Bill puts it, is the importance of their physical surroundings, because the environment is increasingly distant from them. They grow up in subdivisions and in neighborhoods that are isolated from the physical elements, the animals and plants and the surroundings that used to be critical to survival and learning. Perhaps this is inevitable, but it is not something that Bill, Art, T.R. and other longtime Chickahominy residents are ready to accept.

There are increasingly fewer individuals alive who grew up in this culture or remember much about it. There are many books about the life of the Chesapeake waterman, but there are none that examine the unique niche within the bay that flourished along the Chickahominy River. Perhaps not surprisingly, Bill and everyone else who was interviewed are happy to see this situation potentially change, and it certainly was an incentive to interview with the author.

Even allowing for the idealism of youthful memories and the natural human tendency toward nostalgia, there were a number of unique themes in the Chickahominy river community in the 1930s and 1940s. Life was simpler then, and it involved intimate daily contact with the physical environment and the plants and animals that lived within it. It was without a doubt also a hard life. But the hardness was tempered with a beauty that is unmistakable.

CHAPTER 3

CONFLICT AND SOCIAL GEOGRAPHY

The Chickahominy River played a surprisingly prominent role in American history, well beyond the legendary Pocahontas and John Smith. Just after the colonial period, U.S. president George Washington commissioned a shipyard on the lower Chickahominy. Situated on a point where a deep channel made a turn in the river, the area became known as Shipyard Point (also roughly the location of Menzel's Fish House before it was torn down for the making of the Disney movie *Pocahontas*). Sailing vessels were constructed there, and several other small businesses opened nearby.

During the War of 1812, British warships moved upriver and shelled and destroyed the ship works there. According to Bill and others, stories from the War of 1812 abound in local folklore. The point is still called Shipyard Point, and the nearby tributary, Shipyard Creek, but there are no physical remains left. Very close by, at Shield's Point, there was a large house for the manager of the shipyard that was also shelled by the British. Near the house was a small settlement that included a tavern, where Nathaniel Bacon reportedly held secret meetings prior to Bacon's Rebellion in 1676.

During Bill's time, his grandfather and others told stories about "a place to get a drink" and a house of ill repute there. Bill's grandfather also noted this location as a wharf where his red and white oak railroad ties were loaded. When he had enough ties, Bill's grandfather would write to someone to come and pick them up. Bill also remembers the metal *S* rings placed in the ends of the ties to keep them from splitting. Modern saws eventually

A bridge constructed across the Chickahominy Swamp as part of the Peninsula Campaign in 1862. *Courtesy of the author.*

put individuals like Buck's grandfather out of business. But Bill remembers wheelbarrowing two ties at a time to the barge.

Across from Shield's Point is a large rock marking the area where sailing ships dumped their ballast near the south shore. Only a few yards from shore, there is a seventy- to eighty-foot-deep hole in the river channel. Union forage parties passed through here in 1862, "cutting the hams right off the hogs without bothering to butcher them," according to Bill's grandfather.

The Chickahominy region is literally filled with history, and no river played as interesting and as unappreciated a role during the Late Great Unpleasantness (the Civil War) as the lowly, swampy upper Chickahominy. Hardly more than a trickle and an amorphous wetland when its beginnings meander between Hanover and Henrico County, its waters would see the crossing of thousands of Union and Confederate soldiers battling over the fate of the Confederate capital in nearby Richmond, particularly during the Seven Days' Battle and Peninsula Campaign in 1862. As its banks rose during storms, or when bridges were destroyed, the geography of the upper river actually changed the course of history.

Locals, of course, have very little living memory of the events of that time and instead possess diverse socially constructed versions of history that have been passed down through word of mouth and tall tales.

"I don't remember much," Bill said. "My grandparents talked about the raiders that crossed through near the old shipyard…I do remember seeing remains of corduroy and rock roads at the Ferry Landing, which I was told were there when Stuart crossed on his ride around McClellan's army."

Despite the lack of obvious physical remains, few rivers in the South saw as much of the Civil War as did the Chickahominy River in central Tidewater Virginia. From Union general George B. McClellan's famous Peninsula Campaign in 1862 and Confederate general J.E.B. Stuart's concurrent ride around the entire Union army to roving Union gunboats on the lower Chickahominy and marauding deserters desecrating the countryside on either shore in 1864 and 1865, life along the river was completely disrupted for more than four years to a degree unparalleled since 1607 and not equaled since. A few subtle scars of the conflict are all that physically remain today, mostly hidden among the white oaks and old sunken roads of the wood-dotted landscape. But the social, political and cultural impacts remain much more apparent.

Charles City County and New Kent and James City Counties—the southern and northern shores of the lower Chickahominy—provided more than their share of volunteers and other resources to the Confederate cause throughout the war, sending hundreds of young men directly into Confederate service and dozens of others into local duty, like William Collins, of the Charles City Guards, who served in the local militia (and was held in Castle Godwin in Richmond for unstated rules infractions for a short time), or J.C. Vaiden, of New Kent County, who worked at Chimborazo Hospital in Richmond. The local Charles City troops also included such prominent local residents as Captain Robert Douthat, Lieutenant Thomas W. Willcox, Lieutenant Archibald Taylor, Lieutenant Benjamin H. Harrison and others who were well known in the tiny communities surrounding the courthouse.

The area also suffered a disproportionate share of destruction and disruption. Later, there would be numerous reparation claims made by local residents against the federal government for the use of horses, loss of trees, occupation of churches and the seizure of buggies and wagons. Many of these claims were rejected, and those who applied for them were both euphemistically and formally referred to as "Southern Loyalists," terminology that was certain to rub postwar nerves and was subtly connected to the term

"Tories" used in the Revolutionary War. However, the few claims paid out could not come close to mitigating the actual loss of life, physical disruption and collective social disorder that the war wreaked on the region.

The river was (and remained after the war) the primary fabric that wove together the people in the area. In tandem with the nearby James and York Rivers, the Chickahominy River saw mail, livestock, carriage and wagon traffic; fresh fish and seafood; human passengers; and all types of other goods and materials moved up, down and across its channels. Many coach roads in the area terminated at the river, and almost all commerce was directly connected to the river traffic either by the river fords, numerous small wharves, ferries or the railroads that ran near and along the river. Chickahominy boats—part skiff and part flatboat—were moored at nearly every home and at villages all along the river and its many tributaries.

In 1862, when McClellan chose the peninsula between the James and the York Rivers as his advance route toward the Rebel capital in Richmond, the *New York Herald* described the Chickahominy River region in detail for its readers, calling it "now the most important section of the United States concerned in the war" and noting that it provided "extensive water power" to the area. The paper reported that both New Kent and Charles City Counties had populations of roughly six thousand, approximately half of whom were blacks. Three important bridges crossed the Chickahominy along the roads connecting to Richmond: Bottom Bridge, the Long Bridge and Jones' Bridge. Bridges would be key in the coming battles.

While New Kent County, James City County (north shore) and Charles City County (south shore) provided more than their proportionate shares of support to the Confederate cause, the truth is also that these locales were completely rural, with no centralized population centers and no heavy industry. Even Williamsburg of colonial fame, along with Jamestown Island, was in disrepair and neglect. The Governor's Palace and the former capitol building were lonely ruins. Jamestown Island was used as a parade ground and camp to drill troops. Most communities along the Chickahominy were tiny collections of residences around a general store and/or a post office, almost always situated at a crossroads (like Riddle Shop, for example, which was located where the modern Route 5 and the road to Malvern Hill intersect and where a minor battle was fought in 1864). These tiny communities were interspersed with large plantations along the rivers and, farther upland, midsized farms. Other crossroads communities included places such as Adkins Store, Cedar Grove, Binns Hall, Parrish Hill, Ruthville and Wayside.

There were native Chickahominy Indians and free blacks interspersed in certain parts of the counties, many of them near or along the river. Even the courthouse building in Charles City, one of five in America dating back to the Revolutionary era still extant in 2009, was not within an incorporated area or a "town" per se in 1861 but "just around the bend" on a dirt road leading to Richmond (now the aforementioned Virginia State Route 5). The courthouse, which consisted, in part, of "Flemish bond, rubbed brick, and gauged brickwork in segmented arches," survived the war and is an invaluable historic monument.

The war swept through the Chickahominy region like a whirlwind. Former U.S. president John Tyler attended the state assembly as the Charles City, James River and New Kent Counties representative. The assembly drafted the state ordinance of secession on April 17. Registered voters in Charles City County voted 311 to 1 in favor of leaving the Union on May

The Mechanicsville Road bridge over the Chickahominy, circa 1862. *Courtesy of the Library of Congress.*

Woodbury and Alexanders Bridge. *Courtesy of the author.*

A bridge over the Chickahominy during the Civil War. *Courtesy of the Library of Congress.*

23, 1861. Young men immediately flocked to recruiting events at Charles City Courthouse and New Kent Courthouse, first meeting and rousing the local militia and later eventually joining Confederate service through the war bureaucracy of Richmond.

Frank A. Ammons, a young laborer in Charles City, was typical. He rushed to enlist in Company K of the Virginia Fifty-third Infantry, under Captain George Wadill, which gathered on Jamestown Island in late spring of 1861. His regiment would eventually be part of Armistead's Confederate Brigade, in Pickett's Division, a unit made immortal at Gettysburg on the third day during Pickett's Charge. Surviving this and other battles, Ammons returned to live in Charles City after four years of Confederate service. He later applied for a Virginia pension based, in part, on a bullet wound received during his wartime service.

Ammons's story was familiar, and patriotic Confederate enthusiasm spread like wildfire through the Chickahominy region early in the war. Isaac Christian, a candidate for state senator, told his constituents along the river as he campaigned:

> *Virginia will carry with her the border States, and when they, with her, shall have added eight more stars to the flag at Montgomery* [a reference to the early and first capital of the Confederacy in Alabama] *then will the question of peace or war, of prosperity or depression have been settled.*

Cheering rallies gathered regularly during this tumultuous period. It would not be long, however, before the harder face of war came to the Chickahominy.

In May 1862, Union general George B. McClellan, the "Little Napoleon," implemented a massive campaign to move the Army of the Potomac up the peninsula between the James and York Rivers and end the war by capturing Richmond. In order to reach Richmond, a Union army of more than 100,000 soldiers would sweep northwest through Chickahominy country. On May 5, McClellan's campaign to and through the Chickahominy region began well enough with a victory at Williamsburg, with the army and its various parts creeping forward from Fortress Monroe and capturing the former colonial capital of Virginia. The plan had all the promise of ending the war, and some Union outposts would eventually be within sight of the church steeples of Richmond.

Part of McClellan's operation required a detailed reconnaissance up the Chickahominy River. Two warships, the *Island Belle* and the *Stepping Stones*,

A grapevine bridge built in May 1862, by the Fifth New Hampshire Infantry under Colonel Edward E. Cross during the Civil War's Peninsula Campaign. *Courtesy of the Library of Congress.*

were sent more than forty miles up the river to gather as much intelligence as possible. Part of their report of May 28 stated:

> *We passed through some magnificent scenery…overhung with precipitous banks clothed with dense wood, with a rich, undulating country beyond…and occasionally we caught glimpses of extensive fields of wheat…Sometimes, too, we encountered a strip of low, marshy land, overrun with rank, coarse grass, while the broad leaves of the water lily grew plentifully far out into the stream.*
>
> *Farmhouses and private residences were constantly in view, and from nearly every inhabited dwelling a white sheet, tablecloth, or anything that could be extemporized into a flag of truce…I need hardly say that white men were hardly to be seen, as most of them are either with the rebel army or have been killed off in the struggle their leaders have provoked. A great number of houses were shut up, without the least sign of inhabitants in or around them.*

A view of the upper Chickahominy during the Civil War era. *Courtesy of the Library of Congress.*

> *After running up a considerable distance we came upon a log house, built on a steep slope. There we saw a white man, who met us on the landing in front of his house. Above, on the high bank, were two grown white females and two or three white children. The man told us that we could run twenty miles further up, and that we could obtain a pilot at "The Shades." He said he had been forced into the rebel army, but that he had deserted, not liking the service, as he was no believer in secession.*

The sailors, like McClellan and the men in his army, were confident that the end of the war was near. But fate was not on McClellan's side. Instead, the Chickahominy was the river that crowned two new Confederate stars, each of whom brightened the possibility of a rebel victory. Both General Robert E. Lee and J.E.B. Stuart "cut their teeth" in the actions along the river and, as a result, were later immortalized for their military acumen.

The change in the tide began on June 1 at the Battle of Seven Pines, fought a mere dozen miles or less from the outskirts of Richmond, where Confederate general Joseph E. Johnston was wounded and replaced by the relatively unknown Robert E. Lee. Lee began his tenure as commander in chief by ordering a detailed reconnaissance of the enemy, turning to his eyes and ears, cavalry leader J.E.B. Stuart. "You are desired to make a secret movement to the rear of the enemy, now posted on [the] Chickahominy," Lee wrote to Stuart on June 11, 1862. Stuart took Lee's words literally and sprang into action with roughly twelve hundred of his most fit troopers to find out everything he could about the current disposition of McClellan's army and, if possible, to disrupt rear areas and destroy communications. Lee was determined to go over to the offensive rather than let McClellan besiege the capitol.

Stuart's ride began along the marshy banks of the upper Chickahominy but quickly took him eastward into the rear of McClellan's sprawling army and supply network. Between June 12 and 15, Stuart and his men rode nearly three hundred miles in a complete clockwise circle around the Union army, spreading destruction and confirming that McClellan's army was split in half by the swollen Chickahominy. Lee summoned Stonewall Jackson with reinforcements from the Shenandoah Valley, even as McClellan confidently ignored the warning signs that he was no longer fighting the Fabian and predictable Joseph Johnston.

"Once more within our lines," a trooper of Stuart's wrote.

> *All merry as a marriage bell...We have burned two hundred wagons... sunk three large transports, captured three hundred horses and mules... brought in one hundred and seventy prisoners...three million cannot cover the Federal loss!*

McClellan wrote to President Lincoln on June 18, 1862, "Our army is well over the Chickahominy...we shall fight the rebel army as soon as providence will permit." But Lee boldly planned to attack the half of McClellan's army that was physically separated from the other half by the swampy, rain-swollen waters of the upper Chickahominy with superior Rebel forces. Although the initial attacks failed on June 25, for the next week through July 1, Lee hammered McClellan's larger army in a series of attacks known as the Seven Days' Battle. On the twenty-eighth, McClellan wrote to Lincoln darkly, completely changing his tone: "Jackson is driving in my pickets...on the *other* side of the Chickahominy...It is not probable that I can maintain telegraphic communications more than an hour or two longer."

McClellan's army suffered a great defeat, Richmond was saved and Robert E. Lee's star rose, leading the *Richmond Enquirer* to say of Lee: "We are proud of the pure patriot and modest general who has thus unhorsed the boasted 'Young Napoleon.'" But more significantly to citizens of the Chickahominy region, the world was turned upside down. There were dead horses, unburied corpses and burnt bridges. Homes and official buildings were destroyed (although it was Stuart, ironically, who had fired the New Kent jail so that the grain there would not be captured by Union soldiers). According to the *New York Herald*, Haxall's House at Harden's Landing in Charles City County, which had served as a hospital after the Battle of White Oak Swamp and was close by McClellan's headquarters on June 30, was now essentially an abandoned abattoir. The trash associated with a retreating army, including brand-new weapons and food, was scattered everywhere along the roads.

The fighting during the Seven Days' Battle was unusually fierce, due in part to the swampy and irregular nature of the upper Chickahominy. "We drove the Yankees from tremendously strong positions of their own choosing, at the point of the bayonet," wrote a member of the Hampton Legion fighting across the Chickahominy. At one point, Lee had the mill dams above the Bottom Bridge cut, forcing even more water into the swollen river.

"The Chickahominy can scarcely be called a river," one Yankee wrote with disgust.

> *Its proper designation is a swamp, with several channels running through it. Its width varies at different points from two to three hundred yards to a quarter or half a mile. It is skirted on both sides with trees, and in some places is completely overgrown with them, so that it is impossible to see across.*

Nonetheless, his comments clearly indicate the role the river played in foiling McClellan's plan.

Though the Peninsula Campaign and Seven Days' Battle was the most dramatic and large-scale operation along the Chickahominy, the fallout from the conflict never really left the area. Even before McClellan's army departed, many records from the Charles City Courthouse were strewn through the nearby woods in a dramatic rainstorm; those in New Kent County were totally destroyed (first by Union raiders and then

Picket duty along the Chickahominy during the Peninsula Campaign. *Courtesy of the author.*

Scenes from the Chickahominy during the Peninsula Campaign. *Courtesy of the author.*

the remainder in 1865, when Richmond burned). Later in 1862, the Reverend F.B. Converse, evangelist, reported that he was "constrained to leave" his religious work due to the proximity of Union forces, which occupied Williamsburg from September 1862 through the remainder of the war.

Even carrying into 1863, the *Richmond Sentinel* reported that "the York River railroad...in New Kent County...was recently destroyed by the Yankees, and as they carried off the iron, no attempts have been made by the company to reconstruct it, owing to the scarcity of that article." There were numerous accounts of runaway slaves, escaped Union prisoners and deserters being arrested or caught in New Kent or Charles City Counties. On December 13, the *Charleston Mercury* reported that two companies of Confederate cavalry were captured in New Kent County as part of the cat-and-mouse warfare that continued in the region. Although McClellan and the Army of the Potomac officially left in the summer of 1862, the war never did.

There were, of course, no paved roads at the time, and one could easily get lost. Lewis Jester, a writer for the *Richmond Times-Dispatch* and a Chickahominy native, told the following story in 1944:

> *One night three federal soldiers staggered up to the door of a small house near the Chickahominy. An old lady was alone...afraid...and promised anything she had if they would go away. "We want to get out of this God-awful place!" Needless to say, they were told how to get to the road* [and] *got back to McClellan's army.*

By 1864, as Lee was forced onto the defensive, Union cavalry increasingly raided areas away from the main armies. Charles City and New Kent Counties were particularly vulnerable as small rural counties that had already provided well more than half the eligible male population to military service—including many who would never return—and there were few resources away from Lee's Army of Northern Virginia to be spared by the government in Richmond. In March 1864, rumors swirled that Union general Benjamin "Beast" Butler had sent men into New Kent, and they were wreaking havoc in hamlets like Burnt Ordinary, Cole Ford or at Tunstall's Depot. Later in the spring, Grant's massive Army of the Potomac traversed the area, crossing the Chickahominy at the Long Bridge on the way toward the James River and, later, Petersburg. These combined activities further wrecked the region.

Shelling Rebel positions across the Chickahominy River. *Courtesy of the author.*

The Charles City Courthouse in 1864. *Courtesy of the Library of Congress.*

The ruins of buildings near Charles City Courthouse in 1864 (the courthouse survived). *Courtesy of the Library of Congress.*

"We had a fight last Tuesday in which Townson Vass, a boy who has recently joined us was killed," a Union soldier wrote home. The Battle at Kennon's Farm in Charles City on May 26, during which Vass was shot mortally in the right side, was one of countless skirmishes during Grant's movement. The stragglers, deserters and rear guards following Grant's army were even worse. On June 17, 1864, the *Richmond Examiner* reported "an act of brutal lawlessness committed by the enemy in New Kent County." The rape and abuse of a number of young women in the area sent Confederate authorities into an uproar.

When the war was over, like many Southern regions, the Chickahominy region was depopulated, sometimes lawless and subject to Union occupation and military rule. Disabled veterans returned home to find no work available and lands subject to federal seizure. Women, children and the elderly congregated in extended homes for protection and to share resources.

Current longtime residents of Charles City, James City and New Kent Counties have living memories of grandparents and great-grandparents who survived the war.

"Oh, there were stories," Bill Buck said again. "I don't know that they can be verified. But...we all knew about J.E.B. Stuart's ride and that many homes were burnt. We heard stories about gunships coming up the river."

Today, Charles City, James City and New Kent Counties are making efforts to preserve the history of the period. Although the wooden bridges are gone, many of the homes destroyed and all of the dirt lanes paved over,

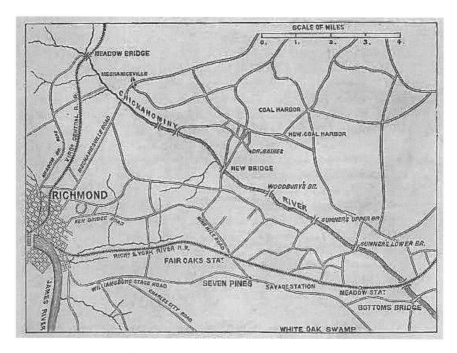

An enlarged portion of a contemporary newspaper map of the Chickahominy River in 1862. *Courtesy of the author.*

The Chickahominy River behind the train tracks at Lanexa, Civil War era. *Courtesy of the author.*

the biggest artifact—and the most important one—remains much the same as it was in 1861. The Chickahominy River lies ubiquitous, patient and sublime, and it defines the area today much as it did back then.

Like many places in the South where the opposing armies battled, the environment near and along the river was literally scoured. Homes were burned, crops destroyed or confiscated, families were displaced, bridges were demolished and railroad tracks were pulled up, laid down and pulled up again. River traffic was often interrupted by Union raiders or naval patrols. Animals were hidden in swamps and specially chosen pastures to avoid seizure, and root cellars were camouflaged. Gardens, too, were moved as much out of the line of sight as possible. Gold, silver, family jewelry and cutlery were buried in the ground (not necessarily the best idea in the Chickahominy region, where a high water table and humidity can lead to rapid decomposition of almost anything).

The memory of those times is a collective experience still passed down from one generation to the next. It is also a memory that merges historical truth and collective memory of truth—fraternal perhaps, but far from identical twins.

"I heard about the war from my relatives long before I learned about it in school or read about it in books," Bill remembers. "That's the way we learned."

"There are all kind of Civil War stories," T.R. said, implying much more.

"If only the river could talk," Bill said. "It could tell you a lot more about the Civil War than I could."

CHAPTER 4

JOURNEY ON THE WATER

Bill is one of the few individuals in the Chickahominy region now living who can say that he made his living solely on the water during long phases of his adult life. Guide, PhD, professor and certified and licensed captain Art Conway is another such individual. The full-time waterman as sole proprietor is a dying breed in the present age in the Chickahominy River area, as well as in the entire Chesapeake Bay region. Most current watermen, like Conway, have other jobs that they maintain during the week or at seasonal intervals. Conway, for example, is a retiring biology professor at the nearby Randolph-Macon College, a short distance north of the Chickahominy headwaters.

Many older residents in the Chickahominy region remember the days of Menzel's Fish House, Henly Jones commercial fishery at Barrett's Ferry, fishing camps for herring or shad dotting the banks and the heavy traffic of commercial vessels along the river. Even younger locals have heard the stories and can repeat them to the curious.

"Mrs. Jones [at Henly's] can skin catfish almost as rapidly as one can count them!" locals bragged. Jones shipped fish all over the eastern seaboard.

"My dad and my granddad told me how they used to catch turtles in the river," Edward, a twenty-year-old Randolph-Macon College student and native of the New Kent County (north) side of the Chickahominy explained. "They would take them all down to Menzel's and sell them."

"It was big business," Bill confirmed.

They would put them whole right into the boiling water, then cut their heads off, remove the lower plate, fold their legs over the eggs if they were female, and pack them up. They went onto a truck that went nonstop to Chicago. [Bill smiled.] Don't ask me what they did with them in Chicago. But I know what my mother did with them.

Bill explained the technique. His father would bring home a big snapping turtle—usually twenty pounds or more—cut its head off and let it bleed into the grass at the edge of the yard, and then his mother would boil the whole turtle. Next she would cut the meat out into reasonable-sized chucks and boil them again. Finally, she would take the chunks out, bread them, season them and fry them in fat.

Bill grinned again. "I still like turtle a great deal!"

Some fishermen constructed their own turtle ponds, where they could hold several hundred at a time prior to shipping. Many other families worked harvesting turtles—the Bradby clan (Chickahominy Indians), Bill Skillman, the Darnell brothers—but very few turtles are harvested for food from the river now. Like other forms of commercial fishery, the turtle industry has simply withered and faded away. Many of the current bass sports fishermen—a significant force of men and women on the river regularly—wouldn't even know how to prepare or cook a turtle even if they happened to be able to get one into the boat without losing a finger or two.

Bill remembers going down to the old fishing camps. There were boats for rent, bait for sale and lots of people interested in making money or taking money from the unwary. The shad camps are in ruins now. But back in the day, people could come in on the train to Lanexa, rent a small shack or cabin and stay in the camp. There were enough shad for everyone.

"Those days are over," Bill said for emphasis.

Many who formerly made their living on the water in the bay region have gravitated to other water communities. Recently, a captain in Rhode Island with experience in the Chesapeake region spoke in an interview about the dying culture of the waterman as he prepared a New England–style clambake for visitors:

Even here [in the New England coastal region, a traditional seafaring community], *people just don't make a living that way anymore. I do this mainly for fun for the tourists, and I don't really make any money from it. I can't keep up with the cost of it for the returns I get.*

Bill Buck, Art Conway, Captain N.N. and many others have experienced firsthand making their living on the water. For Buck, this first happened on the Chickahominy with his family as he grew up in the 1940s; later, it included a career as a commercial captain on the James River, as well as the Chickahominy, and ownership of a larger commercial boat. It later included writing about working on the water and passing on his knowledge to others. Although he gave up officially making a living on the water in 1982, the experience further cemented his unbreakable ties to the water and, particularly, to the Chickahominy.

"I worked on the James River for a long time, too," Bill recalled. "But I always loved the Chickahominy. I ended up back there, of course." Bill paused and looked out across the Chickahominy. "The James is not this pretty."

Lewis Jester wrote in 1944 about Montague Thompson, the "King of Gordon's Creek." Montague was typical of many residents along the river—he was a hunter, trapper, fisherman extraordinaire and loved the Chickahominy. "He still can outpaddle and outwalk any of his city friends," Jester wrote of the older Montague.

An abandoned shad fishing shack along the lower Chickahominy. *Courtesy of the author.*

In his day, Buck made a living fishing, as his father, uncle and others had done before him. Conway inherited the trade from his father, as well. In Buck's case, this often involved catching and selling catfish by the pound to Menzel's Fish House.

"I remember in 1980," Bill recalled,

> *I was setting a few catfish pots in the Chickahominy in the early spring. I discovered a gravel bar up in Morris Creek and set a trap there. When I pulled the trap it was full of white cats; one hundred pounds or so. A good catch for one trap. My uncle told me to set two more traps, and when I pulled all three, found them to be also full of white catfish. This went on for two to three weeks—and then nothing. The buyer said, "What a catch!" Little did he know what was to come.*

According to Lewis Lester, catfish was sometimes sold as "whitefish" for diners at fancy East Coast restaurants and hotels. Locals, however, often preferred it prepared in a stew: "In a big kettle…[with] braised bacon, potatoes, onions, catfish, salt and pepper."

"There were a lot of hard men on the river," Bill said in an interview. "Someone told me that Roscoe had been fishing my pots. You just don't do that! Well, my buddy and I waited in the woods. We scared him pretty good. There were no more problems after that."

Bill and other commercial fishermen have tried to teach me the basics of the trade in the process of my researching the industry. I learned how to set crab pots, how to arrange a fyke net (the kind that Bill and T.R. raided for fish in their youth), how to let out a drift net and where to place catfish pots. According to friendly feedback, I'm still not very good at the cast net.

"Throwing a cast net takes a lot of practice," Bill wrote in his notes.

> *If your neighbor is watching, they may think you are a nut, but you are learning a valuable skill for a fisherman.*
>
> *Attach the line to the wrist; gather the net; swing slowly outward with grace and release; let the net settle to bottom; then jerk the line attached at the risk to close the net around your catch. If you hold the lead line in your teeth as some do, always remember to open your mouth. The secret is practice.*

At one point in his commercial days, Bill was fishing almost two hundred catfish pots and could check about fifty in a single day.

"You would tar the catfish pots every spring before you set them," Bill said. "Typically they would catch catfish up to ten pounds in size. You would place about five of them for every hundred foot of line."

He used trot lines.

Uncle Penny taught me how to make and set trot lines. It's a long line with fifty to one hundred hooks attached from dropper lines. Uncle Penny also taught me some good places to set these. With two trot lines and a Chickahominy boat, I went into the catfish business.

He has also used his own fyke nets that would catch almost anything that swam up and down the river, including very large ring perch. Fyke nets would often be left in place for all of spring. Drift nets and cast nets were also employed depending on the fish being targeted.

"There aren't any hangs in this stretch," Bill said, scanning a section of water that used to be fished heavily. A "reach" was a straight segment of river that the fisherman knew fairly well and was free of snags. The fisherman, sculling with one hand in the back of the Chickahominy boat, would use his other free hand to let the drift net out, zigzagging up or down the river, depending on the tide, and letting the current actually pull the net into the proper position across the river.

"If you do this right," Bill said when we set our net, "the current and the fish do all the work for you. The net just drifts with the river, so to speak. There's an art to it, of course."

Reaches were named locally: Uncle Neck Reach, Bush Neck Creek, Stave Landing Reach, Hog's Neck Reach, Old Neck Reach, Penny's Reach or Turner's Reach. Many don't appear on modern maps with their 1930s and 1940s names.

During the same period, finely crafted silk linen nets were used; they required careful maintenance but performed well if properly stored and dried.

"A net might last three times if you were lucky, if you didn't dry it properly," Bill said.

It was very lightweight. Five pounds of silk net was a lot of net. There were nails in all the walls along the river where people hung their nets.

During the winter, we would hang the nets and stretch them. We spent a lot of time making sure the real cork floats were arranged right—if they weren't placed and secured properly, it wouldn't float right and you wouldn't catch anything. We also would make sure all of the metal ring weights were tied on the bottom.

One of the few remaining commercial fishermen still to be found on the Chickahominy. *Courtesy of the author.*

Many of the materials and tools used by fishermen were made locally. The Ideal Fishing Float Company, for example, was located at 2001 West Franklin Street in Richmond and supplied many items for Bill's fishing business. Bill still has odds and ends manufactured by this company left over from the 1950s and 1960s. The company, like most water-related businesses from the period, no longer exists.

Nets were expensive, relatively speaking, and were treated with great care.

"I remember Daddy waving his cap wildly as we were motoring up the river," Bill said. "'Don't mess my nets up!' he was yelling."

Bill, Art and the other watermen made it clear in their interviews that watermen have almost as much work to do when they aren't fishing as they do when they are actually catching fish. The rituals associated with soaking the Chickahominy boats, maintaining expensive nets, sharpening blades, mending pots and replacing rope were consistently emphasized across accounts.

"You've got to have some kind of love for it in this day and age," Captain N.N. said. "Otherwise it is too hard and pays too little."

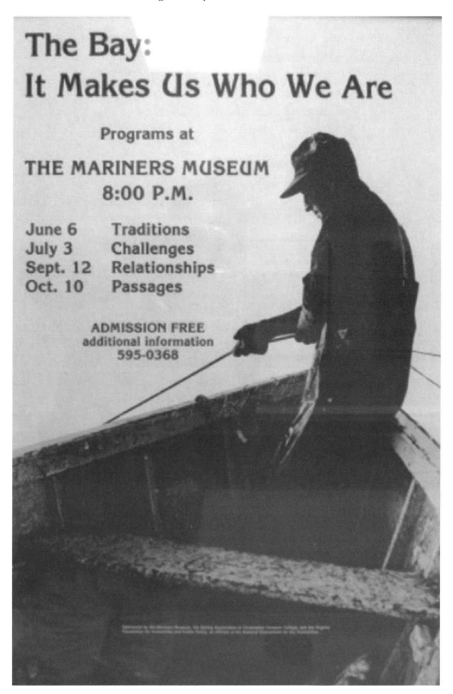

The culture of the bay is endangered, and organizations like the Virginia Foundation for the Humanities try to preserve it. *Courtesy of the author.*

Not so, apparently, in the 1930s and 1940s along the Chickahominy. "If my catch was big enough," Bill recalled,

> *I rode my bicycle to the country store and sold it for five to ten cents per fish. Later, if I was catching fifteen plus fish a day—some in the ten-pound range—then I would go off to Menzel's for the delight of four to ten cents per pound. I was rich in many ways then.*

Many others were also in the same business.

"The nets would be so thick through here that you could almost step from net to net on the corks," Bill said when asked how many people were fishing. In fact, tugboats that moved barges up and down the river would blow their horns at every turn in the river so that fishermen could take their nets up out of the way. Many boats, including the tugs, burned coal for power, and older residents or watermen remember catching or finding "clinkers," or pieces of mostly burned coal, in their nets or along the shore.

Before the dam was built, shad camps dotted the riverbanks. Word of mouth spread like wildfire when the shad entered the river.

"When the shad came in," Bill recalled, "it happened downriver first. My uncle had a small place down the river, and when they came in that was the first place we would go. When they moved to the ferry, we would set our nets at the Ferry Reach."

Buck explained to me that shad were "roes" and "bucks" (females and males), and when you had a net full of them, you had to quickly sort them out and grade them. Shad are a delicate fish and can't be handled as roughly as other fish. Wooden fish boxes, designed expressly for that purpose, could hold up to 150 pounds of shad and would quickly fill up. Currently in Virginia, there is no permitted harvesting of shad in the Chickahominy.

"The females don't lay their eggs in nests," Bill explained. "They just lay their eggs in masses, and the males come by and fertilize them."

There is no question that the Chickahominy was a thriving water-related enterprise in the near and distant past. During the 1870s and 1880s, commercial fishing and water-related business expanded so quickly along the river that the federal government supported dredging for commercial access and produced a river report in 1889 with additional recommendations. As part of this, a detailed survey of the area was conducted and submitted to Congress on November 30, 1889 (pursuant to the 1888 River and Harbor Act), by Mr. S.T. Abert, United States agent.

Reading this report now, a number of important facts about the Chickahominy *then* are revealed. For example, the report and proposed project included "removal of snags, trees, stumps, and similar obstructions." The upper Chickahominy was and remains today unnavigable due to such obstacles. The report also noted that since 1875 "bars had been removed from the lower part of the river" and the work "is now completed." The report also makes reference to the canal near Providence Forge, "cut in colonial times by the British Government, as a means of transporting the Virginia tobacco." Accordingly, boats tried to make use of the old canal rather than the impeded river channel nearby. Since the value of timber transported on the river was approaching $1 million, or roughly $20 million in today's money, the cleaning of the channel would likely increase that value significantly. The report listed that six to eight lighters were engaged in transporting wood and railroad ties to schooners lying at anchor farther downriver (this was the business that Bill's grandfather conducted). The improvement was approved.

By the 1930s and 1940s, the commercial traffic had reached a zenith. Bill, and young men like Art who were born in other areas of the bay, grew up

The author learning how to set nets, check pots and "read" the water. *Courtesy of Captain Art Conway.*

A crab pot on the
Chickahominy.
Courtesy of the author.

in a culture that emphasized hard work and the life of the waterman. For
Art, that career began right away in the family commercial fishing business
in Kilmarnock and continued into the 1970s, when he spent time on the
Chickahominy duck hunting with friends. In addition to teaching biology at
Randolph-Macon College, Captain Conway has been fishing, hunting and,
more recently, guiding in Chickahominy Lake (the section of the river above
the dam) for more than thirty years.

Bill's journey on the water took several detours, including a term of service
in the air force, where he was a specialist handling nuclear weapons loaded
onto B-52s, and time working for NASA afterward. But Bill was never far
from the river, and he had a home and personal wharf there, as well as a
greenhouse business beside it. In the 1980s, he bought a large vessel, the
Pristine Mistress, and began chartered trips up and down the James River. Bill,
Art and others (like Captain N.N.) obtained their captain's licenses, as well as
maintaining the appropriate fishing licenses and permits.

Not as many in the pot as there used to be. *Courtesy of the author.*

Doing more research on the river with Buck and Captain Conway. *Courtesy of Captain Art Conway.*

The *Pristine Mistress* was forty-five feet long and eighteen feet wide and drew four and a half feet of water. It could hold up to forty-seven passengers. Bill's business was called Virginia Charter Cruises, Inc.

> *I took that boat all kinds of places, from Evelynton Plantation, Busch Gardens, Flowerdew Hundred, Hopewell, all the way up to the fall line in Richmond. I took all kinds of people on it. That was a boom or bust time. You made all sorts of money during the summertime. During the wintertime you put it all back into the boat.*

Art mentioned the same thing in an interview: "It [the boat] was a large black hole into which you poured large sums of money."

"Boats are worse than *any* sports car," Captain N.N. confirmed.

While captaining the *Pristine Mistress*, Buck learned much more about the water and captaining a boat that supplemented the knowledge of his youth.

"It was a big boat," he said in an interview. "Compared to what I had steered, it was a little bit different. I learned lots of things by experiencing them, rather than reading a book."

He learned, for example, how to study the clouds and read the wind. He also learned more about human nature and the foibles of Murphy's Law. He learned that you can never predict what will actually happen. Once, his cousin saw a whale in the James River and wanted to shoot it with his 30-30. The U.S. Coast Guard persuaded him not to. But you could never tell what would happen on the river.

"I got a call once about a thunderstorm coming in behind us, and for our own safety I decided to turn around and head back to the marina. But the storm came up on us out of nowhere, and I realized that we weren't going to get back." Bill paused in recounting his story.

> *When the captain gets scared, or when the captain starts seeing things, then I suppose that is the time to worry. But I put the blinds down so the passengers couldn't see the river and the seven-foot swells, turned the throttle into the wind and we made it back. There were some people who got sick, mind you, but we made it back.*

Like the Chickahominy, the James River was heavily polluted in the 1970s and 1980s.

"You could see just about anything on the James floating," Bill recalled. "I saw a monstrous tire that was twelve or thirteen feet tall sticking out of the water—you could get killed by the dang thing."

Even while Bill was busy making a living on the James, he remained tied to the Chickahominy, where he had family land, a wharf and a twenty-four-foot boat that he used for fishing.

"I built that pier," Bill said on a trip to the site. "That is Buck's Gut over there, and this is what I called Deep Landing. This was where I raised seven kids. My best bird dog, Duke, is buried right over there."

Between the 1970s and the present, the remaining commercial fishing on the river simply evaporated. In 2008, only one commercial fisherman spent continuous time on the lower river with pots and nets. The area where Bill formerly lived was representative of this on a visit we made there together. Trees and small pines had overgrown the area, the wharf was sagging and missing boards and the driveway was overgrown and eroded. Even Bill had difficulty locating where a hothouse for plants had formerly been.

But he has no difficulty recalling the days when business was brisk along the water:

A boat similar to a Chickahominy boat in action on the river, circa 1940. *Courtesy of the CCHC.*

Captain Conway on the move. *Courtesy of the author.*

All that is left of an old fishing camp. *Courtesy of the author.*

The tugboats would steam up and down the river all the time, and we would sometimes have to pull our nets out of the way. Sometimes they would stop, and we would trade them a bushel of white perch for a bushel of apples.

"I just want [this] recorded, so it doesn't get lost," Conway said. "A lot of my dad's stories were erased from my memory during my surgeries, and it really hit me that all of this history will disappear with my (and Bill's) generation."

Change, of course, is inevitable. But the life of the Chesapeake waterman—and, specifically, the life of the Chickahominy waterman—is special, unique and worthy of preservation. Individuals like Bill and Art are the fragile vessels in which those memories remain alive and can still be captured.

"We see the health of the river," Bill wrote in his notes. "It is not as Captain Smith saw it. With time comes progress, and with progress comes the failing health of a river. It is still a beautiful and wonderful place."

CHAPTER 5

EVOLVING ENVIRONMENT

The Chickahominy River—the "sportsman's paradise…known to relatively few but the natives"—of Lewis Jester's 1944 report is now a microcosm of the environmental challenges that America faces in the new century. It remains both a tremendous natural resource and a resource damaged by the activities of man. The river has seen many changes since the natives first lived along its banks, and in particular, modern pollution has left its scars on the environment just as it has on many other North American rivers.

According to the Virginia Department of Environmental Quality, more than 1.5 million people live within an hour of the Chickahominy River watershed. Most of these people are unaware that the freeways they traverse, the strip malls where they shop and the storm drains they live near all filter into the Chickahominy. Most are also probably unaware how drastic the changes along and in the river have been.

Some of these changes are measured in numbers and hard data, such as those gathered by the U.S. Geological Survey (USGS). But much of the change can also be measured through ethnographic processes. T.R. remembered when the sturgeons in the river were stacked like corpses on wharves, ready to be shipped to New York to be made into dog food. The roe (caviar) was often thrown away. Some of the sturgeons were longer than the johnboats tied up near them.

Bill remembered the frogs. In the 1940s, there were so many frogs that he clearly remembers being able to paddle through the lily pads and grab them by hand, by the dozen. There are still frogs, of course, but the lily pads are gone, and the frogs are not nearly so easy to find and are apparently present in much smaller numbers.

T.R. remembered the snakes. They were common everywhere, particularly water snakes and black snakes. Stories about snakes dropping from limbs into Chickahominy boats passing by have now become legend. Today, the snakes are not nearly so prevalent.

Bill, Art and many others remember the 1970s, when people wondered if the yellow perch population had been destroyed for good. It seemed a certainty that the commercial fishery for them would never come back to flourish like it had in Bill's youth, and even sport fishing was an open question.

Chickahominy natives spoke of water clarity, or the smell of the water, and shook their heads when asked about the change. "The river has been dead in my time."

"The Chickahominy was so clear," Buck recalled, "you were able to see a fish in the drift net ten feet down."

Many remember a year when the salt water moved so far upriver that it killed bass, and jimmy crabs came farther upstream than they had ever been. According to witnesses, crabs were caught in large numbers right up to the dam.

The *Richmond Times-Dispatch* reported in 1944: "The Chickahominy marshes, swamps and creeks constitute a sportsman's paradise that is known to relatively few."

But in the present, everyone believes that the river has changed.

One of the most perplexing mysteries, as far as locals are concerned, is the sudden disappearance of hundreds of acres of lily pads along the river, particularly below Walker's Dam. Where did they go? In the early to mid-1990s, the pads simply vanished and haven't returned since.

"What has happened to them?" Bill wrote in his notes. "Old-timers say this has been due to the boat traffic. Some people claim it's the incursion of salt water."

Many possible explanations have been put forth: traffic from bass boats, backwashes from hurricanes with unusually heavy tides, storm floods or even grass carp that rooted them up. The consensus among more knowledgeable sources is that a catastrophic physical event of some sort would be necessary to uproot the plants. My theory of pollution was quickly disproven, since water pollution should not impact rooted plants to that extent. Scientists from Virginia Commonwealth University, when queried, could not agree on a likely answer either. No one knows for sure.

No mystery is as great as the disappearing lily pads. Why did they disappear in the 1990s? *Courtesy of the author.*

"We fished those pad fields with ten- to twelve-foot cane poles," Bill recalls. "We baited with soft or peeler crabs. Channel catfish love the crabs."

But the pads are gone now.

The health of the Chickahominy River, like the Chesapeake Bay into which it flows, is a matter of grave scientific and environmental concern to many people, including the federal government. The USGS has been monitoring key water quality factors in the Chickahominy River for decades, and a survey of its data reveals that the health of the river has fluctuated. Like almost all other eastern U.S. rivers, the Chickahominy has suffered from heavy industrial pollution, as well as agricultural runoff, and efforts have been made to work in conjunction with the U.S. Environmental Protection Agency to clean the river and its tributaries.

A tributary near a Tyson chicken plant was recently identified under the Clean Water Act as being degraded by "excess levels of phosphorous," which impairs benthic macro invertebrate communities. State efforts to clean the area and company changes resulted in improvements by 2004, although it seems unlikely that this is an isolated incident. Many of the Chickahominy's smaller tributaries are largely unmonitored.

Some Chickahominy River species, such as the small whorled pogonia and the sensitive joint vetch plant, remain on state and federal protection or endangered lists. Other species, like bald eagles, have made notable comebacks in the area. Even so, the state and federal governments have issued warnings about eating too many fish from the river, primarily due to residual mercury levels, PCBs and other toxins.

The Chickahominy remains premier duck hunting territory for hunters and photographers. *Courtesy of the author.*

Bald eagles have returned to the Chickahominy, the James and other eastern Virginia rivers. *Courtesy of the author.*

"On this side of the dam, the fish taste like stumps," Jerry Adkins says.

There is even a local fisherman's phrase that refers to bass in the Chickahominy as "stump bass." When the salinity of the river changes rapidly, certain species of fish like largemouth bass can't even survive. The bass population plummeted in the 1980s, reaching a low in 1997, and a change in salinity is sometimes blamed for this. Salinity changes are often related to storms, tidal variations and possibly climate change.

"A sign of the times," an old river fisherman shrugs. "Change is inevitable."

Although largemouth bass have made a comeback since 2005 (thanks in part to supplemental stocking and an exceptional 2005 year class), the disappearance of large fields of lily pads, above all of the other changes, continues to perplex many observers. The river was once known for these vast fields of yellow pond lily accompanied in many places by pickerelweed. Most of the pads disappeared around or just before the turn of the new millennium. USGS water quality and water flow records for the last fifty years do show some fluctuations—high mercury levels in the early 1990s, for example—but no single factor that would account for the disappearance of the pads.

"Disappearance of emergent vegetation is most often tied to fluctuating water levels or a big flood," Professor Chas Gowan of Randolph-Macon College said recently. But there are no records of either of those type of events, according to both USGS data and eyewitness reports.

"I was around for Hurricane Isabel," Art recalls, "and things did get stirred up. I remember islands of pads and marsh floating around after Isabel. But there were still pads."

"I was told about a marsh that moved from one side of the river all the way to the other after a hurricane," Bill recalled. "I didn't know whether to believe it or not."

"That marsh right there," Art said, pointing to what appeared to be a little island near the marina, close to some large cypress, "that was not here until after the hurricane."

There is also endless debate about the impact of the dam on the river. The completion of Walker's Dam, which created Chickahominy Lake in 1943, severely interrupted many long-established natural patterns. In fact, some older locals who can remember the river before and after the dam mark its completion as the major turning point in the river's environmental history.

The low-head dam was originally constructed by the U.S. War Department as a saltwater intrusion barrier, according to Brian Ramaley of Newport News Waterworks. Perhaps of equal importance, the dam ensured adequate strategic water supplies for the vital Newport News Shipbuilding and Drydock

Walker's Dam at eye level. *Courtesy of the author.*

Urban development along the lower Chickahominy. *Courtesy of the author.*

A sign warning local inhabitants of malaria risk near the dam in the 1940s. *Courtesy of the CCHC.*

Company. The roughly four-hundred-foot concrete dam connected the New Kent and Charles City banks and originally included twin Denil fish ladders (which yellow perch reportedly use, too) for anadromous species, as well as a boat lock that could accommodate vessels up to almost forty feet long. In present times, the dam ensures a water supply for almost half a million civilian customers in the tidewater Virginia region.

Chickahominy Lake, created above the dam, is approximately twenty-two miles northwest of the confluence with the James River and consists of more than twelve hundred acres. The lake has become the site for a number of small businesses as recreational use of the lake steadily increased over time. Of course, commercial traffic and larger commercial businesses on the river that were stymied by the dam and quickly died out have not returned.

In 2007, the dam failed. Though studies in the late 1980s and early 1990s indicated that large numbers of shad were passing over the dam, it is not so clear that fish patterns have remained stable. It is also not clear what the long-term effects of the dam have been on migratory fish patterns and water quality. During the time the dam was breached, tides ran in and out of the lake, and saltwater intrusion had an impact on the food chain in the lake.

"The shad fishery is dead," Buck says. "I don't mean that you can't find some shad, but the fishing camps are gone, the shad run is gone and the days of filling wooden fish boxes up with hundreds of shad are gone."

"You don't find [the shad] in the lake," Captain Conway said. "When the dam broke and the lake became tidal again [in 2007], it definitely changed things. The fishing was strange, for lack of a better term. It was different."

The dam has since been repaired, but the experience while it was broken—in combination with the memories of old-timers—combines to make a statement. The construction of the dam *did* change the river. Perhaps not for the better.

For Bill Buck and many others who remember or know of the old Chickahominy before the dam, memories are still vivid and tinged with sadness over the passing of an era. These memories include crude fishing villages, now overgrown and vanishing in the trees, water-related industries like the brick factory where bricks were loaded onto barges bound for various destinations, a colonial-era shipyard or even fishing for eels under the lily pads with a simple piece of string and a thread.

"You could fill the boat up with them," Bill said. "Do you want to try it sometime? Now that the pads are gone, though, I'm not absolutely sure where to go to do that…I don't catch many eels anymore."

In former times, Bill would catch hundreds of pounds of eels at a time to sell, as eel was an expensive table item in major eastern markets. Lewis Jester recounted how eels would chase carp literally out of the water in former days. But not anymore.

And there is ample evidence that the water is significantly different. The USGS data provide evidence of this. Some of the facts include unusual lows in cyclical dissolved oxygen levels in the mid-1980s and again as recently as 2007–08, high mercury levels in the mid-1980s and into the early 1990s and residual toxic contamination from PCBs and similar pollutants.

Some things are also obvious from anecdotal evidence. Most species of fish are not as big on average as they used to be. Personal accounts and state fishing records support this notion. In the 1970s, there were six-foot sturgeons in the river. Bill remembers a man named Horace catching a huge sturgeon in a drift net near the bridge at Barrett's Ferry. Now, the sturgeons are smaller and sometimes difficult to find in the river. In the past, there were weekly bass tournaments and regular ten-pound largemouth caught. Ed Allen (George Allen's son, who took over the family fish business that failed when the dam was built) runs a marina and restaurant on the lake and has hardly seen a ten-pound fish in the last decade like he used to on a fairly regular basis.

"The most striking difference is in the fish," Laura Helmuth wrote recently in relation to fish photos as environmental artifacts. "They get smaller and fewer, and species disappear with the passage of time." Though Helmuth is

The fish really were bigger in the good old days, according to photographers and research. *Courtesy of the author.*

Bill saw Horace Binns dragging this fish back to his wharf (he couldn't get it into the boat). It's a six-foot sturgeon, circa 1940s. *Courtesy of the CCHC.*

writing primarily about the sea, she makes clear in her introduction that the same applies to freshwater species. "The historical records reveal astonishing declines in most fish stocks."

Bill Buck and others concur. "Oh, there is no question," he said. "The fish were much bigger when I was growing up, and that's not just a fisherman's tall tale."

"All of the species across the board were much bigger when I was younger," T.R. said, agreeing.

When I asked Art about my quest for a fourteen-inch yellow perch in the river, his reply indicated the same: "They probably exist, but I haven't seen one over thirteen yet in the lake." Captain Conway has fished commercially and served as a guide for dozens of years, including more than thirty in the lake portion of the Chickahominy.

Some fisheries nearly disappeared. The ring perch, for example, was wiped out in specific bay areas by large, sometimes unexplained fish kills. In the 1970s, Bill and others notice a precipitous decline in ring perch size and numbers in the Chickahominy. In the last decade, however, they have made a comeback of sorts. People know intuitively that things are happening in the river's biological web, but they can't always identify macro and micro effects without formal scientific investigation.

"We used to catch big croakers along here, and sea trout," Bill said.

Some fisheries seem to increase, while others decreased. During the 1970s, crab harvests remained very strong, even in the face of known pollution and environmental change. Bill remembers catching up to fifteen or twenty bushels of crabs a day during this period of time. Before Labor Day, he would sell them for twenty-five dollars a bushel, and it was a full-time job checking more than 150 crab pots regularly.

Why did ring perch decline, while crab populations remained strong? There are reasons, of course, but the bay is incredibly complicated, and studying one part of it in detail often reveals very little about how the entire system functions in an integrated fashion. The answers remain elusive.

According to the Chesapeake Bay Foundation:

> *The rare crayfish snake has been spotted along the* [Chickahominy] *River and, although most of the Chickahominy watershed has not been thoroughly surveyed, scientists suspect the habitat is right for other rare reptiles and amphibians as well.*

There are possibilities; there are threats.

A wild relative of the rhododendron, which Bill's father called ivy. *Courtesy of the author.*

The same might also be said of plants. In 1941, M.L. Fernald and Bayard Long recorded finding and preserving a specimen of *Micranthemum micranthemoides*, a rare mud flat plant, along the Chickahominy River on the "fresh tidal shore…above Lanexa [*sic*]" (and before the construction of the dam). According to Susan Milius, this is the last known sighting of the specimen, and it may now indeed be extinct. (In fairness, Milius also reports that Larry Morse recently rediscovered a plant thought to be extinct along the Chickahominy, *Bacopa stragula*.)

Complicating matters are foreign species that have been introduced. The blue catfish is now sought after as a sport fish by some but is not native to the river. It is accused of contributing to the reduction of largemouth bass populations in the late 1980s and early 1990s. Blue catfish, introduced with good intentions in the 1970s, have had an impact on other catfish species, as well, likely reducing channel catfish populations (which are also nonnative and were introduced in the 1890s) and certainly reducing the average adult size of channel catfish. Blue catfish also graze on zebra mussels, which are positively correlated to healthy yellow perch populations. The infamous snakehead fish has made its appearance in

Cypress and their roots dominate the waterline scenery along stretches of river. This tree is on Parsons Island, where the old cypress that was struck by lightning when Bill was a child is still present. *Courtesy of the author.*

bay waters, including rivers like the Chickahominy (anglers must report when they catch one).

The ice is also a mystery. The river hasn't frozen over in more than fifty years, and yet many longtime residents remember it happening fairly routinely back in the day. Is this due to the dam? Global warming? Saltwater intrusion?

Ed Allen, whose father was a commercial fisherman and who now runs a marina and restaurant, says that the lake itself has changed over time:

Pickerelweed. *Courtesy of the author.*

One thing a lot of people don't know is that the lake doesn't freeze up any more. I've seen people drive a car across this lake. When I was a kid, we always packed up and went to Florida every winter when the lake froze. I believe the warmed climate has an effect on the grass…the cold doesn't kill it back so bad.

"Most people who live and work in the watershed are highly sensitive to its tenuous situation," environmentalist Sara Lewis wrote earlier in 2009, "located as it is between city and country lifestyles…The Chesapeake Bay is polluted and many of its species are threatened…[The Chickahominy River] is threatened by development and water withdrawals for drinking water."

Parts of the river are also designated as scenic waterways and have forest and wildlife preserves contiguous to them. These factors should help offset many competing negative variables, like housing and commercial development. They should, in theory, make it easier to protect what is there and possibly restore what is in danger of being lost.

There is no question among the eastern Chickahominies or the residents who grew up on the river in the 1930s and 1940s—change seems to be occurring regardless of attempts to slow it down. On a recent trip along the river to complete a map of his experiences, Bill took the boat by a new housing development right along the river. The houses were very nice homes, most in excess of three to four thousand square feet, all with elaborate docks and wharves. All were built within twenty to thirty feet of one another and right on or *over* the water.

"I suppose they're nice homes," Bill said slowly, clearly implying at least four or five other unspoken opinions about what was *not* nice about them.

By one way of thinking, these residents are just another wave of the constantly changing river culture. They will have their own love of the river, their own stories and their own history to hold on to. They will have their own children, some of whom will grow up and leave and others who will stay and make a life near the water.

"At least they're not polluting the river," I said to Bill, trying to be positive.

"They are pollution," he responded. "Eye pollution." After a pause, he asked, "How many of them do you think understand the life cycle of the crab?" (This was a reference to *Beautiful Swimmers*.)

It is hard to begrudge people their chance to live on a beautiful river. Nonetheless, I am forced to agree that I would rather see fields of Indian oats, banks of cypress and lines of pickerelweed than row upon row of brand-new houses.

It is also fair to point out that the river was not a riverine utopia in the 1930s and 1940s. Boats, when deemed un-repairable, were allowed to sink where they were, including many barges that gradually sunk into the mud beside channels. Some of these boats contained oil, gasoline and other chemicals that would eventually be released into the river. To keep the channels open to boat traffic, the channels were frequently dredged, a process that had sometimes dubious effects on water quality and microscopic elements of the food chain. Many businesses dumped directly into the river—there was no EPA or DEQ playing the role of watchdog. Menzel's Fish House routinely dumped the offal from its fish cleaning right back into the river.

There is also the fact that the entire Chickahominy watershed, filled as it is with marshes of various types and sizes, is an incredibly important protection device for the surrounding ecosystems. According to a 1980 College of William and Mary report:

> *The beautiful wetlands areas found in much of this section of the Chickahominy River* [the tidal estuary; the lower third of the river] *and its various tributary creeks are some of the most valuable natural areas found anywhere along the James River drainage.*

These areas are the breeding ground and nursery for many species of waterfowl and fish, as well as incredibly diverse plant life. They are often "dominated by vast stands of arrow arum." "Unfortunately," the report continues, "contamination by the pesticide Kepone currently makes many of these species [of fish] unsuitable for consumption."

The marshes and tidal flats remain essentially giant filtering systems at the end of the river in spite of the pollution. Unfortunately, the report notes, more marshland was destroyed with the construction in 1978 of a dam across Little Creek, a Chickahominy tributary in James City County near the old colonial shipyard (again by Newport News Waterworks).

Farther up the river at Chickahominy Haven, near Big Marsh, additional damage has been done:

> This section marks one of the wetland areas…that have been impacted by man's activities. [The] year-round residential community includes a number of dead-end, dredged canals that are…a source of poor water quality. Poor tidal flushing within the canals combined with runoff of fertilizers from the lawns and gardens, drainage from septic tanks and fecal matter from household pets produce…water that is of low oxygen content but high coliform count.

Chickahominy Haven is directly across the river from Old Neck—in other words, a stone's throw across the river from the big white house where Buck grew up. Interestingly, when the College of William and Mary report came out, there were still many lily pad fields in the river.

It is hard to talk to longtime residents and to spend time in the community and on the water and not come away with a heightened sense of concern about the environmental health of the river. The rusting crane at the end of the old brickyard pier attracts many photographers because of the impressive osprey nest on top of it. This crane is both a symptom and an irony. It provides a good home for one of the most impressive birds on the river, yet it is also rusting, oxidizing and releasing pollution into the river. No one would dare take it down because of the nest—but should they?

There are more questions than answers.

How should development be monitored? Counties need a reasonable tax base to support services, but too much growth strains the environment.

"Nobody would buy this land along the river in the old days," Bill said. "They said the river was inaccessible. Now I can't afford to have land on the river."

Rose mallow. *Courtesy of the author.*

Local administrators such as Stran Trout, New Kent county supervisor, have been trying to walk the fine line between commercial interests that benefit the county and preservation that takes a longer outlook. The Chickahominy Water Trail project, still in planning, is an effort to collaborate with the National Park Service and a larger Captain John Smith National Historic Trail.

According to Bill, this is the size fishermen liked to get in their catfish. *Courtesy of the author.*

"The Chickahominy River's vast marshes and swamps act as huge natural filters," the draft text reads, "removing pollution from the water...even when the rest of the James River has been engulfed by polluted runoff."

The Chickahominy, however, is not immune to the effects that trouble the James River and other bay tributaries. On the contrary, there is evidence that its very remoteness has worked against it receiving the protection and care that it deserves.

CHAPTER 6

THE YELLOW PERCH

The ways of the perch are well worth learning!" wrote biologist Frank Thone in 1930, referring to the yellow perch. "When he comes to the table, he can hold his head and tail with the most aristocratic of them!"

Perca is the early Greek word for "perch," and *flavescens*, the Latin word for "becoming gold colored." No single species of fish tells the story of the Chickahominy River better than the story of the yellow perch. The yellow perch has countless local names all over North America and Canada: American perch, bandit fish, calico bass, convict, coon perch, coontail, Eisenhower, jack perch, jumbo perch, lake perch, perch, raccoon perch, red perch, redfin, redfin trout, ringtail perch, ringed perch, river perch, sand perch, striped perch and yellow ned. It has been successfully introduced in seemingly obscure places, such as reservoirs in Nebraska or South Dakota. Among the Chickahominy watermen, the fish is commonly called simply a ring perch. I prefer to call it yellow ned.

Ring perch is a vividly colored fish, with a compact oval-shaped body ideally suited for the cool, clear water in which it schools and feeds. In the Chickahominy River and Lake, it commonly has a deep green back, ranging into golden brown along the sides, interrupted by seven dramatic, tapered vertical bars, or rings. Along the belly, it is white, with bright orange anal fins, particularly colorful on the male. Photographs and illustrations do not always do the Chickahominy ring perch justice; its colors are striking, lush and tropical, particularly among breeding males.

The ring perch is slightly humped behind the head compared to other relatives, with two separated dorsal fins, the first spiny-rayed and the second soft-rayed. The anal fin has seven to eight rays. The ring perch also has additional scales extending from the gill flap that differentiate it from some of its bass cousins. Its appearance is streamlined, and fishermen value its relative strength compared to other fish its size, although some will argue that the ring perch doesn't fight as hard as other bass cousins (it so happens that I disagree with this—a citation ring perch can pull a pole).

Ring perch feed on "immature insects, larger invertebrates, fishes and fish eggs during the day." They are prey for other fishes and various waterfowl. According to Susan Luna, they have a moderate to high vulnerability to drastic environmental stresses like pollution and under ideal conditions can live to be eleven years of age or more.

Ring perch are "random" spawners, and when the water temperature cools enough (in Virginia usually in February, about forty-six-degree water temperature), females move en masse to deposit their eggs in gelatinous strands. Up to two dozen males follow behind fertilizing. On the Chickahominy, the largest spawning takes place just below the dam. Unlike other relatives, the ring perch has no nest (like bass) and no parenting or protection of the young. Under normal conditions, surviving young grow to three to five inches in the first year or so.

In Maryland and Virginia in the Chesapeake Bay region, yellow perch have traditionally grown very fast (with some notable exceptions in the second half of the twentieth century). In the Chickahominy Lake and River, adult ring perch commonly range between six to twelve inches in length, with the river below the dam generally holding larger fish. The Virginia Department of Game and Inland Fisheries (VDGIF) citation program recognizes any fish twelve inches or longer as a citation fish. Some states have a fourteen-inch citation (a very large ring perch). However, Bill and many old-timers along the river remember when two- and three-pound ring perch ranging to sixteen inches in length were commonplace. The longest recorded length anywhere is twenty-one inches.

"We'd pull them up in the nets fairly regularly," Bill recalls. "Sometimes there would literally be hundreds of pounds of them. We didn't think anything of it and would throw them back sometimes. But that all ended by the '60s and '70s."

According to Paul Piavis:

Commercial yellow perch fishing is a difficult endeavor. Tending fyke or hoop nets set in the Bay and tributaries during March requires smaller open

This is the largest yellow perch the author has seen in person—thirteen and a quarter inches long. *Courtesy of the author.*

Yellow perch commonly grew to two pounds (and larger) in the 1930s and 1940s in the river. The same has been reported in the past in other bay rivers as well. *Courtesy of the author.*

boats with outboard motors. Combine these with wind, icy decks, flowing tides and numb fingers, and one can imagine how yellow perch fishing requires a certain breed of waterman.

Ring perch seemed almost to disappear in the Chickahominy between the 1950s, when there were several newsworthy ring perch fish kills in bay rivers, and the 1960s and '70s, when pollution and toxins reached their peak levels. Not surprisingly, the river's famous largemouth bass population also declined precipitously during this period, much to the dismay of regional anglers. In the 1990s, the ring perch made a comeback in the Chickahominy and many other Chesapeake Bay river watersheds, but nowhere has the ring perch returned in the numbers or sizes relative to the first half of the previous century, when the fish supported a thriving commercial fishery in tidal rivers all around the bay, from Maryland south to almost North Carolina. Some Maryland rivers are still closed to recreational and commercial harvesting or limited to five fish per day.

There is, of course, a widespread recognition that the bay is still in danger, despite some recent small victories.

"The bay is in trouble," Chesapeake Bay Foundation president William C. Baker wrote recently.

> *Entire species of fish are no longer commercially or recreationally viable. And others are just hanging on…Toxic chemicals, sediment, and nitrogen and phosphorus…fertilizers, auto emissions, and more. We are paying the price.*

Bill Buck, though far from an eco-terrorist, is sullen about the changes that he has witnessed along the river. "Who knows what's actually been dumped in here."

But researchers do know. The VDGIF knows, too, and it has posted signs along the river that warn fishermen not to eat what they catch. For all of the ring perch's innate natural beauty, there is a hidden inner toxin that it carries for its entire life. When it dies or is eaten by predators, those toxins remain in the food chain. The toxins seep into the sediments of the river.

Native Americans, particularly of the local Chickahominy tribes, also have noticed the changes.

"It was the dam," one tribe member stated in an interview. "Before Walker's Dam was built, that river was clear as a glass of water. Now it's murky and dirty. The dam ruined the river."

Presently, the ring perch appears to be regaining population strength in the Chickahominy, but disaster is only one season away. Scientists monitor bay fish for "strong year classes," which indicate the relative short-term health of a population. One bad season can set a threatened species back several seasons and put the entire population at risk.

Bill has his own system for monitoring the health of the Chickahominy ring perch. As a master angler with more than ten citation ring perch caught in the river and lake, he is a relative civilian expert on the ring perch.

"It's my favorite fish," he says unabashedly. "They have personality. And very few people appreciate their beauty or their angling pleasure. It seems to me that they are slowly coming back. Nothing like the old days of course, but better than it was."

According to Bill and other seasoned anglers in the mid-South, yellow perch love water temperatures around sixty-eight degrees, give or take a few degrees. Buck has kept detailed fishing logs since the 1980s, including water temperatures for fish caught, and the collective data for hundreds of ring

A citation yellow ned from the lower Chickahominy River. *Courtesy of the author.*

perch catches confirm this suggestion. Buck, the master angler for ring perch, has come to love yellow neds after years of fishing for many other species, both commercially and recreationally (he last won a bass tournament in 1981, more than twenty-eight years ago).

Using his logs for a series of years, peak fishing times on the lower river seem to be in the months of September and October, as the water slowly cools. The numbers of fish caught per trip in the mouths of creeks and in the guts farther up the creeks double and triple in these months.

In many ways, the yellow perch is a bellwether species for the river, rising and falling with the quality of the water. Few anglers fish just for them, but all anglers and individuals sympathetic to the environment should logically be concerned about them. In spite of near record numbers caught in the lake on Captain Conway's numerous trips, population sampling by the state in 2006 through 2008 suggests that the lake is not overflowing with large yellow perch. Only four citation ring perch were caught in the lake in 2008, and the longest fish sampled in that period by the state was ten inches (two inches below a citation). Below the dam, more citation perch have been caught (many by the author and Buck), but still not in the quantity of former days.

Like largemouth bass, yellow perch are sensitive to salinity levels and amounts of submerged vegetation that foster the foods they prey on. According to the Virginia Department of Game and Inland Fisheries,

> *Beds of submerged aquatic vegetation (SAV), critical to the health of the Chesapeake Bay, are much reduced from historical levels...SAV beds provide excellent habitat for young bass as well as forage species.*

In the Great Lakes, yellow perch remains a significant commercial fishery, and in Cleveland, Ohio, a yellow perch sandwich is a local specialty. In many northern states, particularly along the Great Lakes, research is regularly conducted on the health of the yellow perch populations. Lake Erie probably has the best-known commercial fishery for yellow perch.

Bill and I conducted research together on yellow neds between interviews and other work. While I facilitated what I officially called an ethnographic interview, Bill documented his ring perch fishing in a carefully maintained fishing log that included every fish caught, the date, the weather and other pertinent information. In the process of my research, I have also taken up ring perch fishing and begun submitting my own citations for certification as a master angler. We both have been reading continuously about ring perch, and on one particular morning, as we launched the boat, we shared the most recent results of what we've found with each other.

"I read in the *In Fishermen* that the temperature is the key," Bill explained. "Anything above seventy degrees and you can forget it. They'll be in the deeper water."

"I read that they rely on vision to feed," I said. "They are inactive at night, and feed primarily in the morning and late afternoon."

In North Carolina, anglers fish for raccoons using crickets on the bottom with a float on the top. They are characterized as "notorious bait-robbers."

On the dozens of trips that I make to the river and spend on the water, I learn many of the areas that Bill, Captain Conway, N.N. and others consider good spots for yellow perch. Bill, for example, has caught citation yellow neds off of the Cypress Banks, an impressive area with sandy, cliff-like banks and cypress trees. Bill jokingly referred to Cypress Banks as the "Grand Banks" of the Chickahominy.

Captain Conway knows many ring perch hot spots on the lake and frequently guides fishermen to catches of two dozen or more yellow neds. Like Buck, Captain Conway keeps a meticulously detailed fish log and reports regularly on fishing in the lake for the *Richmond Times-Dispatch*.

Though a longtime angler myself, I sometimes found myself caught up in the excitement of the chase after yellow neds.

On May 29, 2008, I recorded in my field notes:

> *The river is absolutely gorgeous today…Clear, cool, crisp, sunny bright, calm, smooth, reflective, green, alive. Summer is literally in the spirit of the water. If we don't catch a lot of fish today, a couple of citation yellow neds, something is wrong in the cosmic organization of the universe!*

Ring perch range all over North America and Canada and were originally a glacial species. Since then, the species has spread through the Mississippi Valley and down the East Coast. The species has thrived in a variety of environments, inhabiting lakes, ponds, streams, rivers and tidal rivers like the Chickahominy. Usually they prefer cool, clear water, and though they have been known to survive in lower oxygenated areas, they are susceptible to winterkill and pollution. The world record is four pounds, three ounces, caught in Cross Wicks Creek, New Jersey, in 1865. The state record for Virginia is two pounds, seven ounces, and does not seem to be in any danger of being broken.

Like most other river fish, ring perch inhabit different parts of the river during different seasons of the year. They can be caught in shallows at the mouths of creeks on late spring evenings but generally inhabit deeper waters near thermoclines in the middle of the hottest part of the day. In the spring, they are often attracted to structure along steep drop-offs and guts. Later in the summer, ring perch follow vegetation and lily pads that border steep drops. Conventional wisdom maintains that larger fish prefer deeper water, which in the Chickahominy might mean fifteen to twenty feet of water in the river and five to ten in creeks. The drop-offs near guts typically range up to eight feet in depth.

A saying along the Chickahominy goes: "Where you catch one ring perch, there is always another one still there." But part of the ring perch riddle along the Chickahominy is that seldom are more than three or four large fish pulled from any single location at one time, except during the spawn.

As mentioned previously, the ring perch school in the main river for the spawn in the late winter, usually February on the Chickahominy, during which time the females will move northwest toward Walker's Dam and lay long ribbons of attached eggs, which the males follow to fertilize. The adults then leave the eggs to their own fate, and the hatchlings must fend for themselves.

The Yellow Perch

"I've been told that if you can locate them up here near the dam when they come up to spawn, you can catch hundreds of them," Bill said. "But I've never seriously tried to locate them at that time of the year." We looked at each other briefly, and there was the promise of another future project silently agreed upon.

Bill has an evolving science of fishing for ring perch on the Chickahominy that involves some simple guidelines. For starters, you only fish for them in the tributaries and creeks on the outgoing tide.

"Why?" I ask.

"I'm not exactly sure," he says, "but I know it's as true as throwing a light switch on and off. It's just one of those things."

In the lake, of course, the tide makes absolutely no difference in when you can catch ring perch. Captain Conway has proven this in varying conditions, excluding the time frame when the dam was broken and fishing was unpredictable.

Many of the things that I learned from Bill often turned out to have some firm basis in fact and science. When I fished on the incoming tide for hours and caught nothing, I started to believe. When we caught a dozen fish immediately after the slack tide on the outgoing tide, I further believed. After we repeated this experience a dozen times, I *do* believe. (I eventually found out it has to do with the way food travels and cycles in the river food chain.)

"If you aren't catching anything, and it's a spot we know holds fish, you need to fish deeper. Make sure you're getting to the bottom," Bill said.

I catalogued all of Bill's fishing wisdom in my field notes the same way I systematically collected his stories about the river culture. Part of me also wondered why reading it in a magazine or seeing it on a website is never quite the same. Having someone show you how to do it still seems to matter. Practicing it matters. There is also a version of the Heisenberg Uncertainty Principle in play: fishermen often know what ring perch or other fish do, but they don't always know *why*.

The ring perch is carnivorous and therefore a very active fish in pursuit of food. It is almost always an opportunist that may seize the moment when presented with a tempting meal, even at odd times of day.

Another rule of thumb Bill insisted on was using live bait. On every successful yellow perch quest, we tipped our hooks with live wax worms.

"It works," Bill said simply.

Some anglers insist that fish marking with a fish finder is critical: "They will mark as short thin lines, generally no more than a half foot from the bottom."

For anglers of freshwater fish, the approved techniques for netting trophy-size ring perch are fairly simple. Vertical jigging blades tend to work well in deep lakes, such as Lake Moomaw (where the Virginia state record comes from), but in tidal Chesapeake Bay tributaries like the Chickahominy, yellow neds respond rapidly to crappie jigs and spinner combos with live bait, fished at the mouth of creeks and guts in deeper water. In the lower Chickahominy (below Walker's Dam), it is key to fish on the outgoing tide and, when possible, at dawn or in late afternoon.

Bill and I took a liking to the nickname "yellow neds" and began referring to ring perch that way. He can't forget when two- and three-pound yellow perch used to come up in the nets on the Chickahominy River all the time. Those days are gone now. In fact, during some stretches in the 1980s and early 1990s, it was not apparent that the yellow perch would ever thrive again.

There is no detailed evidence explaining the full extent of what pollution has done to the Chickahominy River, but the rise and fall status of yellow perch suggests that pollution is still a major issue influencing fish populations. Government warnings along the river tell anglers not to eat the fish due to mercury and other poisons, and USGS water testing has confirmed the residual presence of various toxins. All of this suggests that the problem may not completely go away any time soon. A drought in Virginia at the turn of the millennium had an impact on salinity and reduced many fish populations, including bass, further complicating the yellow perch's situation.

In the Great Lakes region, the yellow perch attracts a great deal of attention and scientific investigation. One research report details a scuba diving expedition in Lake Michigan to survey spawning areas and to collect very specific data on egg masses. Some of the research is in cooperation with the Great Lakes Fishery Commission.

In the meantime, I have learned to love a fish to which many anglers in Virginia pay little attention, and non-sportsmen and sportswomen, none at all. I love yellow neds.

POSTSCRIPT

I should mention in closing this chapter that Bill, Art and I have become interested in longnose gar fish. Gar are prehistoric in appearance, with a long torpedo-like body and a very peculiar sword-like mouth. They are typically large fish, growing up to three and four feet long. They are not easily caught by traditional angling methods.

One old method relied on a metal wire loop, passed around their snout from above and tightened on contact. Natives also used weirs to catch them. Bill and I have decided to try special lures with no hooks that instead rely on the fish tangling the nylon skirts in its teeth. I recently was wading in the North Anna River and had the pleasure (or fright) of watching three large mating gar fish literally swim between my legs. They were oblivious to me. I could have used a metal loop.

In the Chickahominy, there is an area that has always been known as the gar pool. On our search for yellow neds, we have often spotted entire schools of gar rolling on the surface of the water in the sun. They are often very large fish.

According to the Audubon field guide, gar are "rarely eaten, and the roe is poisonous...There are unverified reports of attacks on humans."

Bill and I have decided that perhaps we will become master anglers of gar fish now.

CHAPTER 7

RETURNING TO ROOTS

Bill now lives farther away from his childhood home, the big white house, but stays very close to the river. His current home in Henrico County, just outside of Richmond, is literally within a stone's throw of where Route 60 crosses the upper Chickahominy. When we passed over the narrow river on a four-lane bridge on the way to the brickyard, I asked him casually about it.

"I guess you've never fished that stretch, have you?" I asked. "Too far upriver…It's pretty rough terrain."

I remember the Civil War stories: "What a hellish piece of insignificant river that's nothing more than a swamp!" many Union soldiers wrote home, describing the upper Chickahominy. I have tramped around the region enough to say that I have been all over the river, and I have ticks, chigger bites and poison ivy to show for it. I am told that I am lucky not to have been bitten by a snake.

"Actually, I have," came Bill's surprising reply. "I've fished it more than once, but I can tell you there's not much there." A wry smile crossed his face. "I like to go where the fish are."

He means, of course, the lower Chickahominy or, on some occasions, the lake. No matter what happens in his work or day-to-day life, he never finds himself away from his childhood haunts for too long. He can't bring himself to spend time on the other nearby rivers—the Pamunkey, for example, where citation ring perch are caught with some regularity. Or even the James, where he worked commercially. There is something about the Chickahominy that is irresistible.

"That river is in my blood," he says, not for the first time.

Captain Conway is similarly unapologetic about the lake. "I like it," he says simply, with a subtle smile. And not only does he like it, but also his more than thirty years' exploring the lake make him likely *the* premier expert on it.

"Do you know much about the river?" I asked T.R. in an interview.

"Everyone knows about that river who lived there," T.R. said, as if my question were a simple one.

However, as the years pass, fewer and fewer individuals survive who *were* there and *do* know something about it. Those who survive are not always willing or able to share their stories. Often, they are not asked. Those who can share, and are willing, are small in number but remain goldmines of memories, special abilities and cultural history. Like the wide-open waters of the lower river, they reflect the times and the events that shaped them the same way the river reflects everything along the shore and sky overhead.

Life along the Chickahominy remains slow and quiet, even with new commercial and residential developments and unexpected environmental changes. It is the nature of the river still and the nature of some of the people who live along it and spend time on it. The Chickahominy First Americans were inextricably drawn back to it—in spite of imperialist colonial policy, racist state policies and persistent economic hardship—and today they inhabit its banks once again. The plantations no longer grow tobacco or wheat, but there are still those who grow cotton and corn and hunt deer in the forests and swamps.

Some groups have made attempts to bring the Chickahominy region back into the forefront. A regional study designed to heighten awareness and provide data for spurring projects was recently completed by the Richmond Regional Planning District Commission. One project includes a capital biking and hiking trail that ultimately reaches the banks of the Chickahominy. A Chickahominy magazine for local residents was in the works until the economic downturn. More signage for Native American and Civil War sites has been discussed. Since the economy slowed, however, many projects and many developments have come to a complete standstill.

A look at the maps produced by the planning commission show a number of businesses and attractions along the river: the Chickahominy Wildlife Management Area, Eagle's Nest (for events and weddings), the Blue Heron Restaurant, River's Rest Motel and Marina, the Chickahominy Tribal Center and Edna Mills all in Charles City County. Colonial Harbor Marina, Rockahock Camping Resort, Ed Allen's Campground and the Long Bride are all in New Kent County.

When the light is right, everything reflects on the river, creating a beautiful mirror effect with sky, trees and water. *Courtesy of the author.*

A drive around the back roads near the river shows many new homes still going up in spite of the economy, some split off from family lands for sons and daughters and some built by transplants and "escapees" lured to the country by trees and freedom. Change is inevitable, and though Bill, T.R. and others are barely retirement age or just beyond (Art just retired in 2009 from Randolph-Macon College), their experiences tie them to a new generation that is submerged in and consumed by "progress." It is a progress that none of them can completely ignore, even if they wanted to, but all feel at least some regret about it.

I find that I regret it, as well. I found in my field notes where I began to fall in love with the idea of this unique culture and this amazing river: "Sun glared rhythm of the boat engine; fishy breeze dried with mature Indian oats—marsh grasses, limp broken straws to stir my summer memories."

Many notes like this—almost poems—appear in my handwriting as the entries and interviews grew in scope and length and began to pile up in boxes.

Bill has also shared his own versions of river poetry. I found this handwritten note of his as I cleaned out my files:

Knowledge isn't a lasting thing, not unless it's written in a good many places. People die and what they learned often dies with them. Whole races of folks that once lived are now gone and what they knew we'll not be able to guess. I can remember the steam engine blowing on a cold morning; the start, noon, and trilling whistle at the brickyard, and lots of things in between.

The river was there long before the first Europeans, it was there well before the first Native Americans and it will still be there when all of us are gone. Some of its geographic features are transitory—for example, the cypress stump remaining on Parson's Island from when Bill was a child will finally rot and fall into the water someday (although it is still there at the moment), and other trees will be cut down, houses will fade into the underbrush, marshes will literally move during hurricanes, the river will change course and even the roads will change course—but the river will outlast them all.

We all agree—Art, Bill, T.R., Chief Adkins and everyone with whom I've talked—that there is something serene and completely sublime about that fact. That is a large part of the attraction of rivers—this river and all such rivers.

"Who owns this river?" I asked Bill during an interview.

Classic Chickahominy River scenery. *Courtesy of the author.*

More research on the river. *Courtesy of the author.*

The end of the day along the Chickahominy River. *Courtesy of the author.*

"No one," he said.

I was actually referring to some marshland when I asked the question—those transitory mud flats that exist one season but are gone the next. How would it be surveyed? Most of it is so wet and marshy that even a sign would sink in it. What would happen when it disappeared? Would you not own it anymore?

But I realized that his answer was important and should stand alone. No one owns the river. This was the concept that the Chickahominies were unable to explain to the newcomers. It is the reason the Chickahominies remained off reservations.

All humans wonder at some point about their own existence and cautiously speculate about what will happen when they are gone. Bill hopes that his story of the river culture will be there for his grandchildren; Art hopes that people will remain connected to the life on the water and interested in its complexities and beauties; the Chickahominies hope to remain near the river and finally be recognized by the federal government for their very identity as First Americans of the Chickahominy. Some, myself included, are simply happy to have discovered the river and especially the wonderful people who lived along it.

Rapid population growth, the advent of new technology and the alteration and exploitation of the environment have all combined to make life appear to be moving at supersonic speeds. Still, the question remains: what will happen when *we* are gone?

No one knows. But the Chickahominy River will still be there. And in some small way, the wonderful and diverse history of the region during Bill's lifetime will still be present, too.

The Ring Perch
(from Maryland DNR)

Kingdom *Animalia*
Phylum *Chordata*, animals with a spinal chord
Subphylum *Vertebrata*, animals with a backbone
Superclass *Osteichthyes*, bony fishes
Class *Actinopterygii*, ray-finned and spiny-rayed fishes
Subclass *Neopterygii*
Infraclass *Teleostei*
Superorder *Acanthopterygii*
Order *Perciformes*, the perch-like fishes
Suborder *Percoidei*
Family *Percidae*, the true perches
Genus *Perca*, the yellow perches

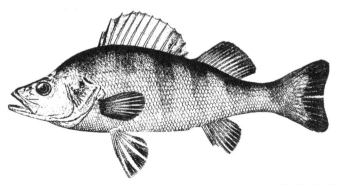

Figure 1. Yellow perch, *Perca flavescens*, about life size, after a drawing by H. L. Todd from Goode (1884-87) obtained from National Oceanic and Atmospheric Administration/Department of Commerce website.

LIST OF INTERVIEW SUBJECTS AND BIBLIOGRAPHY

Adkins, Elaine, and Ray Adkins. *Chickahominy Indians Eastern Division: A Brief Ethnohistory*. Philadelphia, PA: Xlibris, 2007.

Aigner, Terry. "Why Fish and Fishermen Alike are Drawn to the Magical Chickahominy Lake Year after Year." 2006. http://www.highbeam.com, accessed May 3, 2009.

Buck, Bill, Jr. "Collected Fish Logs from 1957 to 2007." Unpublished manuscript, 2007.

"Chickahominy Water Trail Draft Text for John Smith and Chickahominy Exhibits." December 16, 2008.

College of William and Mary. "Rivers and Watersheds: The Chickahominy." http://www.wm.edy/geology/Virginia/rivers/chickahominy.html, accessed June 28, 2007.

Creative Publishing International. *The Complete Guide to Freshwater Fishing*. Chanhassen, MN: Creative Publishing International, 2002.

Galluzzo, John. *The North River: Scenic Waterway of the South Shore*. Charleston, SC: History Press, 2008.

Helmuth, Laura. "Seeing Is Believing." *Smithsonian*. (September 2008).

Hingley, Audrey. "Keeping their Heritage Alive." *Cooperative Living* (June 2009).

Jester, Lewis. "Sportsman's Paradise in the Chickahominy Marshes." *Richmond Times-Dispatch*, September 24, 1944, sec. IV.

Lang, Varley. *Follow the Water*. Winston-Salem, NC: John F. Blair, Publisher, 1961.

Lewis, Sara. "Chickahominy River in Virginia." http://environmentalism. suite.101.com, accessed March 3, 2009.

McWilliams, Dick. "Fishing for Yellow Perch." In *Iowa Fish and Fishing*. Des Moines: Iowa Department of Natural Resources, 1987.

Milius, Susan. "Are They Really Extinct?" *Science News* 161, no. 11 (March 16, 2002).

Moore, Kenneth A. *James City County Tidal Marsh Inventory*. Virginia Institute of Marine Science, William and Mary College, 1980.

Mueller, Gene. "Yellow Perch Hunters Are Finding some Action in Various Tidal Creeks." *Washington Times*, February 25, 2000.

North Carolina Sport Fish Profiles. "Yellow Perch." http://www.ncwildlife. org, accessed November 24, 2008.

Pala, Christopher. "Victory at Sea." *Smithsonian* (September 2008).

Piavis, Paul. "Yellow Perch: Fishing the Spawning Run." http://www.dnr. state.md.us, accessed January 15, 2009.

Richmond Regional Planning District Commission. *Chickahominy River Recreational Access Study*. Richmond, VA: RRPDC, 2007.

———. *James River Interpretive Guide*. Richmond, VA: RRPDC, 2005.

Ryan, David D. *The Falls of the James*. Richmond: William Byrd Press, 1975.

Samuel, R., L. Huber and W. Ogden. *Tales of the Mississippi*. New York: Hastings House Publishers, 1955.

Spradley, J., and D. McCurdy. *Conformity and Conflict: Readings in Cultural Anthropology*. Upper Saddle River, NY: Pearson/Prentice Hall, 2009.

Thone, Frank. "Ichthyology Nature Ramblings." *Science News Letter*, November 1, 1930.

Trammell, Jack. "Down on the Chick." *Virginia Wildlife Magazine* (2009).

Trout, W.E., and L. Stran. *The Chickahominy River Atlas*. Draft manuscript, 2008.

Virginia Department of Game and Inland Fisheries. *Chickahominy Lake 2007*. Richmond, VA: DGIF, 2007.

———. *2009 Freshwater Fishing in Virginia*. Richmond, VA: DGIF, 2009.

Warner, William W. *Beautiful Swimmers*. Boston: Little Brown and Company, 1994.

Williams, James D. *National Audubon Society Field Guide to North American Fishes, Whales and Dolphins*. New York: Alfred A. Knopf, 1997.

Wood, Karen. "'Beyond Jamestown' in Richmond." *VFH Views* (Spring 2009).

WEBSITES

www.alliancechesbay.org
www.chickahominytribe.org
www.dnr.state.md.us/Bay/yperch.html
www.dnr.wi.gov
www.usa-civil-war.com

Primary Interview List

Adkins, Arnette Redwing
Adkins, Chief Gene Pathfollower, CIED
Anderson, Eric
Buck, Captain Bill, Jr.
Conway, Captain Art
Ledbetter, Judith
N.N., Captain*
Pomeroy, Jacqueline
Scanlon, James
Seaton, Mike
Stewart, Assistant Chief Gerald Algie, CIED
Stewart, Jacqueline
Stewart, Sheila Lynn Adkins
Street, Bill
Stuart*
Trout, Stran
Victor*
Wallace, Edwin
W., R.R.*
W., T.R.*

*names withheld at the request of the interviewee

Others Providing Vital Information and Support

Bruce, Jennifer, Randolph-Macon College
Charles City County Center for History
Chesapeake Bay Foundation
Ed Allen's (George Allen's)
Escape Enterprises
Gegugeit, Robert
Mills, Sally, DGIF
New Kent County Board of Supervisors

Randolph-Macon College
Salzman, Randy, *Blue Ridge*
United States Environmental Protection Agency
Virginia Department of Game and Inland Fisheries
Virginia Foundation for the Humanities
Virginia Wildlife Magazine
Virginia Writers Club
Walker, Lee, DGIF

ABOUT THE AUTHOR

Jack Trammell teaches in the sociology department at Randolph-Macon College in Ashland, Virginia. He has written more than seventeen books and numerous articles and stories and writes a regular column for the *Washington Times*. He lives on a farm in central Virginia with his wife and seven children.

Visit us at
www.historypress.net